MW01030911

Children's Stories of the Bible
The Adult Version

Volume 1
The Old Testament

Jack Kelley

PRESS

Dedication

⋯⇒◉⇐⋯

This book is dedicated first and foremost to our Lord Jesus about Whom these stories are written and to Whom all Praise, Honor and Glory are due, and next to my incredible wife Samantha, who was there helping and encouraging right from the beginning and has never lost faith. And finally to Chuck Missler, whose tape series "The E.T. Scenario" persuaded me beyond reasonable doubt that God is Who He says He is, and ignited a passionate study of the Bible that's lasted 20 years now and shows no sign of diminishing.

Acknowledgements

I give thanks to and for my daughters Kecia, Jennifer, and Jessica who have always prayed for me and encouraged me, to my son Benjamin who has brought untold joy into my life, and to Aidan, the son I haven't met yet, who will arrive about the time this book goes to press.

I also owe a debt of gratitude to all those who as sounding boards participated in the Bible studies where the ideas for these stories first took form, to the teachers around the world who have used them for Sunday School lessons and sent messages of encouragement, and to the countless thousands of who've lent financial, spiritual and moral support while visiting our website. We couldn't have done it without you.

Table of Contents

Introduction

The Children's Stories of the Bible are often a child's first glimpse of God, and the simplistic way in which they're told is great for little minds. Recent surveys show that a very high percentage of adults who call themselves Christian still believe these stories from their childhoods to be true.

But most of us have never heard the adult versions with their additional detail and background; information that not only enhances their validity but reveals additional insight into the character of God.

And for non-believers who've relegated them to the status of fairy tales and fables this additional background provides logical and rational reasons to re-think their decision and look at the Children's Stories again. As you'll see they are actual events that describe God's earliest revelation of Himself to man.

Here then are the adult versions of the Bible's Children's Stories, with detail and background to support the fact that these stories aren't just a biblical version of Aesop's Fables. They really happened, and for good reason. Over the seven years I've been studying them I've uncovered a wealth of information, which I've pieced together into my view of the story behind each story. I hope reading them will prompt more intense study on your part, to see if these things are true.

For everything that was written in the past was written to teach us, so that through endurance and the encouragement of the Scriptures we might have hope. (**Romans 15:4**)

Creation Part 1 ...
In the Beginning

⸬═◉═⸬

In the beginning, God created the heaven and the earth. And the earth was without form, and void, and darkness was on the face of the deep. And the Spirit of God moved upon the face of the waters. And God said, "Let there be light" and there was light. And God saw the light; that it was good, and God divided the light from the darkness. And God called the light Day and the darkness He called Night. And the evening and the morning were the first day. And God said, "Let there be a firmament in the midst of the waters and let it divide the waters from the waters." And God made the firmament, which divided the waters which were under the firmament from the waters which were above the firmament. And God called the firmament Heaven. And the evening and the morning were the second day. (**Genesis 1:1-8**)

The Story Behind The Story

I've quoted this portion of the creation account from the King James since that's the way most of us first heard it. Some of the modern translations are a little easier to read but this one is most familiar, and frankly, none of the translations I've seen is really clear.

The first verse is OK, but a quick lesson in Hebrew is helpful. The Bible uses three Hebrew words to describe creation events. *Bara* literally means to create and always refers to a direct work of God. It's the word used in verse 1 and means to make something from nothing. *Asah* means to make something from something else, and *Yatsar* means to form or fashion something as a sculptor or potter might do. Both *bara* and *asah* are used in **Genesis 1:26-27** when speaking of Man's creation, and all three are used together in **Isaiah 45:18** concerning Earth.

Shamayim, translated heavens in verse one, is what we would call the sky. The word is plural because it includes both the earth's atmosphere and the vast reaches of space where the stars and other celestial bodies reside. The Bible distinguishes between the atmosphere and the expanse of space, calling them the 1st and 2nd heavens respectively. The third heaven is of course the Throne of God.

(When speaking of the firmament separating waters above from those below, the Hebrew word is *raqiya*. This is Earth's atmosphere or the 1st heaven. Before the Great Flood, this firmament supported a water vapor canopy that enveloped the Earth and deflected harmful ultra-violet rays preventing them from damaging life on Earth, hence the notion of separating waters above from those below. So the water vapor canopy separated the atmosphere from space; the 1st heaven from the 2nd. It also made for a uniformly sunny sub-tropical climate the world over with no variation in weather patterns. No rain, storms, floods or even heavy winds would have occurred on Earth before the Flood.)

Verse 2 is a horse of a different color. Many scholars believe the verse should actually read, "but the Earth became formless and void, an uninhabitable ruin." Apparently, combining a strict use of grammar with clarifying passages elsewhere in the Old Testament leads to a hint of some sort of judgment between verses 1 and 2 that left the Earth in a shambles, an uninhabitable ruin. The controversy revolves around two issues; a) whether the Hebrew requires an active (became) rather than passive (was) form and b) the Hebrew words *tohu* and *bohu*, translated formless and void. These words are found only in **Genesis 1:2, Isaiah 45:18** and **Jeremiah 4:23.** In the Isaiah passage the Lord reveals that He didn't create the world in vain (the Hebrew is *tohu*) but formed it to be inhabited, thus supporting the idea that it became an uninhabitable ruin. And in a vision Jeremiah saw Earth when it was formless and void (*tohu* and *bohu*) in the context of a judgment.

The Gap Theory

Viewed this way, the first 2 verses of Genesis would go something like this. In the beginning God created the Heavens and the Earth. As you would expect of God, everything He created was complete, perfect and beautiful, ready for habitation. But then something caused a judgment that left the Earth an uninhabitable ruin for who knows how long. It was dark and wet and cold, but the Spirit of God never left the scene, and after some extended period of time, God said, "Let there be light." And so what we know as the Creation account actually begins in verse 3.

This view, known as the Gap Theory, helps solve the so-called "old earth young civilization" problem, and reconciles several other issues between creationists and other scientists. By the way, don't try to use the Gap Theory to explain fossils. Death came into the world through sin, and that came after Adam and Eve arrived. Fossils were formed only once in the Earth's history; during the Great Flood.

Where Did They Come From?

But what could have caused such a judgment? Some rabbinical scholars contend that the way the first letter was formed in the first Hebrew word of Genesis 1 warns us that nothing preceding it can be known. But there are hints that can lead us to informed speculation. For instance, in **Job 38:7** we see the angels shouting for joy at the Genesis 1 creation events. Where did they come from? In **Genesis 3** "the shining one" in the form of a serpent tempts Adam and Eve in the garden. He's described as a created being in **Ezekiel 28:13**, but when was he created? And in **Isaiah 14:12-20** and **Ezekiel 28:11-19** we read of a rebellion and judgment in

Heaven. The King James identifies the one rebelling in Isaiah as Lucifer, and from Ezekiel we learn that he was created as an anointed cherub, in charge of the guardians of the Throne of God, and a visitor in the Garden of Eden. Surely these are references to the rebellion, judgment and fall of Satan, events that began before the creation of man and conclude at the end of the Millennium. Could they have also brought about a pre-Adamic judgment of Earth? Many informed scholars speculate just that.

Speculation? Yes. Will we ever fully understand? Not till we get to heaven. But I think that using the Bible as its own commentary presents compelling, though circumstantial, evidence that favors the Gap Theory. Next we'll look at the length of each creation day, discover why the Jews have always begun their day at sunset and learn when time began.

Creation Part 2 ...
Let There Be Light

A nd God said, "Let there be light" and there was light. And God saw the light; that it was good, and God divided the light from the darkness. And God called the light Day and the darkness He called Night. And the evening and the morning were the first day. (**Gen. 1:3-5**)

Shedding Some Light On The Subject

I've begun this chapter with **Genesis 1:3-5** because I believe this is where the creation account begins. By the way, some ask how there could be light on Day 1 when the sun and moon didn't appear until Day 4. Like so many things, the answer lies in the Hebrew language. The word translated light in verse 3 is *owr* meaning illumination. In verse 14 speaking of the sun and moon the Hebrew word is *maowr* meaning a luminous body, or light repository. The word literally means chandelier. In making the sun and moon, God was gathering the light into repositories that would provide it according to schedule. Note that in referring to the sun and moon the Hebrew word *asah* (to make something from something else) is used rather than *bara* (to create something from nothing). Like a chandelier the sun and moon are not the light itself but were designed to hold and disperse, or reflect, the light.

God Speaks Hebrew

In calling the light Day, He used the Hebrew word *yom,* a word that appears 2244 times in scripture. 1977 (over 88%) of those appearances clearly refer to a 24 hour period. And simple observation of nature tells us that the growth cycle of nearly every living thing is based upon alternating periods of darkness and light in relatively short intervals. Life as we know it could not long exist on any other cycle. This makes the view of long Creation "days" (where years and years of light were followed by years and years of darkness) difficult to imagine. The question is not how could God work so fast, but why did He take so long? Since He could have created it all in the blink of an eye, He was apparently creating a set interval.

Darkness and night are also direct translations of *chosek* and *laylah* respectively, so there is no obvious reason to take any of these words other than literally unless you're trying to reconcile evolution with creation, an impossible task.

On the other hand, the words for evening and morning provide a wealth of information when viewed in the original. Their roots also reveal the reason God began the day at sunset rather than midnight. Dr. Gerald L. Schroeder is a Hebrew scholar with a doctorate in physics from MIT. I had the good fortune to meet him in Jerusalem, where he lives, on one of my trips to Israel. In his book, "Genesis and the Big Bang," Dr. Schroeder explains that according to ancient Hebrew sages, the word for evening, *erev*, comes from a root meaning "mixed up, stirred together, disorderly." It brings to mind the confusion we sometimes experience just at dusk, when the mixed up light and darkness can cause our eyes to play tricks on us. *Boker,* the word for morning, comes from a root meaning discernable, able to be distinguished, or orderly. This word recalls the returning clarity of vision that accompanies dawn.

That's Against The Law

As a physicist familiar with the second law of thermodynamics (the Law of Entropy), Dr. Schroeder was astonished. Simply stated, the Law of Entropy explains that when left alone everything in the universe will deteriorate from order into disorder. For simple examples, just look around you. Even when you apply a regular program of maintenance to retard the process, everything you own, your home, your car, even your own body will sooner or later completely fall apart and stop working. Entropy is a natural law like Newton's Laws of Motion and Gravity and cannot be reversed.

By using these words for evening and morning in their particular order God reveals that in each day of creation He was overruling the Law of Entropy by bring disorder into order. This demolishes any argument that the earth came to be by accident or coincidence, or that man could have evolved from animals that evolved from fish, etc. Such a natural phenomenon is in and of itself impossible, since it requires that nature violate a fundamental natural law. Only the application of an external creative power superior to natural law could have brought about Earth and its inhabitants. To make sure we get the point, God repeated the phrase six times, one for each day of creation, and caused His people to begin their day at sunset. Every day since then the Hebrew calendar has reminded man of God's superiority over the laws of nature, by saying, "First there was evening (disorder) then there was morning (order)."

It's About Time

By the Seventh day, God had finished all the work He had been doing, so on the seventh day He rested from all His work (**Genesis 2:2**). According to some Rabbinical sources, the underlying meaning of this verse explains no less than the beginning of time. Having completed the work of creation and placing man on Earth to subdue and take dominion over it God rested, and in so doing placed in motion all the laws that would govern man's existence, including the duration of the day, the week, the month and the year. These time references were all established during the six days of creation and would remain throughout man's tenure on Earth.

Now you know the adult version.

Adam and Eve

Now the serpent was more crafty than any of the animals the Lord God had made. He said to the woman, "Did God really say you must not eat from any tree in the garden?" (**Genesis 3:1**).

Thus begins the story of Adam and Eve in the Garden, but to get a fuller understanding some observations from Genesis 2 will be helpful.

Whose Story is This?

First, some scholars point to differences between chapters 1 and 2 that hint of inconsistency in the creation account, but there's a simple explanation. The Book of Genesis consists of 10 sections, each the account of a different patriarch but all brought together by a single author, the Holy Spirit, working through the hand of Moses. Each section begins with the phrase "these are the generations"(KJV) or "this is the account" (NIV). Only God was around for chapter 1 but beginning with chapter 2 Genesis describes events from the perspective of Adam and his descendants. Some even assert that Moses had possession of written accounts from Adam and others and drew upon them in compiling Genesis. Since archaeologists have discovered great libraries from pre flood times, this view has merit.

Then there's the comparison of the Hebrew words translated naked in **Gen. 2:25** and **3:10**. In the Interlinear Bible, a direct Hebrew to English translation, the root of the word translated naked in **2:25** literally means to be empty or poured out, or figuratively, naïve or child-like. In **3:10** a different word is translated naked. It comes from a root meaning crafty or cunning, and is used in **3:1** to describe the serpent. Interesting. In their desire to become like God as the serpent had promised, Adam and Eve actually became more like the serpent.

Did God Really Say ...

The startlingly obvious fact that Eve was OK conversing with a serpent tells us more was going on than we realize. The word translated serpent literally means enchanter so what we know about a serpent's appearance was learned after its judgment. I can't imagine any man or woman being comfortable talking with a snake today. The serpent's first question formed the basis for all man's disobedience ever since. It sounds so reasonable but think of all the undermining of His word that begins with that phrase. Did God really say...

Life begins at conception? (**Eccl. 11:5**)

Homosexuality is wrong? (**Rom. 1:24-27**
There's no other God but Him? (**Isa. 46:8-9**)
Don't accept a different Jesus? (**Gal. 1:8**)
We're saved by grace alone? (**Ephe. 2:8-9**)
You must be born again? (**John 3:3**)
The Land belongs to Israel? (**Gen. 15:18-20**)
The list goes on. Get the idea?

There Is A Way That Seems Right To Man But In The End It Leads To Death (Prov. 14:12)

When the woman saw that the fruit was good for food and pleasing to the eye, and also desirable for gaining wisdom, she took some and ate it. She also gave some to her husband **who was with her** and he ate it (**Gen. 3:6**). Her reasoning was good but her logic flawed.

By the way, why did the serpent approach the woman instead of the man? The passage clearly states he was with her. Most of the popular opinions have been offered by men trying to bolster Adam's excuse that it was the woman's fault but here are two reasons, both theologically sound.

1. To bring about the complete fall of man, the woman had to sin first. Had Adam taken the fruit and then given some to her, Eve would have had a plausible excuse before God. "You told me to obey my husband. I was just following your rules." By approaching Eve first, the serpent accomplished the utter fall of both.

2. This is the Bible's first model of the Messiah. Just as the Lord loved you and me so much that He became one of us and gave His life to pave the way

for our redemption, so did Adam love Eve. Stop and think. He was there with her and watched her commit the sin. He could have refused the fruit and remained sinless, but then he would have lost her forever. In joining her in her fallen state he literally gave his life for her and paved the way for her redemption, for from her seed the redeemer would come. From **1 Tim 2:14** we learn that "Adam was not the one deceived; it was the woman who was deceived and became a sinner." So Eve was tricked, but Adam committed a sin of volition, and in doing so chose a path that would make possible her redemption, and ours.

Who Told You That You Were Naked?

Then the eyes of both were opened and they realized they were naked, so they sewed fig leaves together and made coverings for themselves (**Gen. 3:7**). Here is the first act of religion; sinful man's vain attempt to "cover" himself before a Holy God. But God showed them a better way. The Lord God made garments of skin for Adam and his wife and clothed them (**Gen. 3:21**). He was teaching them that it was by the shedding of innocent blood that they would be covered, not by the works of their hands. This event symbolized the coming sacrificial system for setting aside man's sin, another Messianic model. For Christ died for our sins once for all, the righteous for the unrighteous to bring you to God (**1 Ptr. 3:18**).

Now you know the adult version.

Cain and Abel

Adam lay with his wife Eve and she became pregnant and gave birth to Cain. She said, "With the help of the Lord I have brought forth a man." Later she gave birth to his brother Abel (**Gen. 4:1-2**). The Hebrew root for Cain means to procure, while Abel means transitory or meaningless. From Eve's comment and Cain's name we discover that the Lord had delegated the procreation process, enabling obedience to His command to multiply and fill the earth (**Gen. 1:28**) with out requiring a direct act of creation for each person born. We can also assume from Abel's name that she believed Cain would be her redeemer, and therefore felt Abel was unnecessary. (Discovering the meanings of Biblical names can be so fascinating! Whether it's a person or place, you'll almost always gain added insight into the passage.)

Now Abel kept flocks and Cain worked the soil. In the course of time Cain brought some of the fruits of the soil as an offering. But Abel brought fat portions from some of the first born of his flock. The Lord looked with favor on Abel and his offering, but on Cain and his offering he did not look with favor. So Cain was very angry and his face was down cast. Then the Lord said to Cain, "Why are you so angry? Why is your face down cast? If you do what is right will you not be accepted? But if you do not do what is right sin is crouching at your door; it desires to have you, but you must master it (**Gen. 4:2-7**)."

Everything Written In The Past Was Written To Teach Us ... Rom.15:4

Here we learn that the remedy for sin was first taught to Adam in the Garden, not to Moses at Mt. Sinai. By offering the firstborn from his flock Abel illustrated the concept of innocent blood shed for the remission of sin, a model of the Messiah, while Cain brought the works of his own hands, an offering of thanksgiving. Because the Lord reminded Cain to "do what is right" it's clear that He had instructed them on this. The sin offering, an act of confession, purifies us and permits our reentry into the presence of God. Only then will our offerings of praise and thanksgiving be acceptable. Formalized in the Levitical system, and simplified in **1 John 1:8-10** this was actually revealed at the instant of the first sin. It demonstrates our need for a Redeemer while teaching the futility of either providing our own remedy for our sins or ignoring them altogether (as Cain did) both of which are actually offensive to God.

Confess Early And Often

Now Cain said to his brother, "Let's go out into the field." And while they were in the field, Cain attacked his brother Abel and killed him. Then the Lord said to Cain, "Where is your brother Abel?" "I don't know," he replied, "Am I my brother's keeper?" (**Gen. 4:8-9**)

As was the case with his father Adam the Lord asked Cain the question, not because he was seeking information, but because He was seeking confession. Adam gave a flimsy excuse (it was the woman's fault) but Cain showed callous indifference. In fact, isn't it hard to see anything good in Cain's behavior? He ignored the Lord's command about offerings and then became angry when his was rejected. Instead of confessing, he let his anger become jealousy toward Abel and lured him into the field for a pre-meditated act of murder. Then he lied about it, and expressed only indifference when confronted. Little sins, left unchecked, become big ones (**James 1:15**).

The Lord's warning, "Sin is crouching at your door and desires to have you" bears a closer look. The Hebrew word translated crouching was used in ancient times to describe the way a demon would lie in wait for a victim. Perhaps because of this passage, the word desire is the same one used to describe Eve's attitude toward Adam in **Gen.3:16,** meaning "to long for." Our enemy has a passionate interest in us and will lie in wait, longing for the opportunities presented by our sins. Having failed to apply the prescribed remedy for sin, Cain was fair game and the enemy took full advantage. Please remember,

Cain had a relationship with God, spoke with and was taught directly by Him, and still committed a grievous sin. It's a striking example of the pervasiveness of the sin nature introduced into the human gene pool at the fall, and should remind us all of our tendency toward sin, no matter how "spiritual" we think we are, or how strongly rooted in our faith. (See **1 Peter 5:8** and **1 John 1:8-10**).

The Mark Of Cain ... A Model Of Grace

So Cain was driven from the land to live as a fugitive and vagabond. He was afraid that he would be forever banished from the presence of God and deprived of His protection. "Not so," said the Lord, and put His mark on Cain saving his life (**Gen. 4:15**). The collective mind of scholarship has been probed in vain to determine the nature of this mark, but that's not the point. All through the chapter the covenant name of God has been used, indicating the scope of Cain's relationship with Him. Cain sinned and refused to confess, and therefore put himself out of fellowship with God. But God didn't revoke His covenant, nor did He withdraw His protection. Unconfessed sin interrupts our relationship with God and causes us to wander in spiritual wilderness, but it doesn't sever our family ties and it doesn't put our eternal life at risk.

Cain serves as a model of so many Christians today; out of fellowship for refusing to recognize and confess their sins, but still in the family and still living protected (eternal) lives. Objects of the enemy's passionate interest and fair game for his trickery but marked by the Grace of God as off limits to the Stealer of men's souls.

Now you know the adult version.

Cain and Seth

Cain lay with his wife, and she became pregnant and gave birth to Enoch. Cain was then building a city and he named it after his son Enoch (**Gen. 4:17**). Technically this account is not a children's story but a fascinating continuation of Cain's life from which we can draw much insight.

There is a principle in Biblical interpretation called "first mention." It's not a big deal but when you go to the place where important ideas first appear and read the passage in context, you'll often pick up additional understanding. For example the first appearance of blood (**Gen. 4:10**) is in connection with Abel's murder and introduces the idea that life is in the blood. In **Gen. 9:4-6** this is expanded into instruction on proper meat eating (another first mention) and capital punishment (still another). Placing the blood of the lamb on their door posts preserved life for the Israelites at the first Passover, and the ultimate importance of this idea lies in the phrase "saved by the Blood of the Lamb." His life exchanged for ours.

My Three Sons

The idea first mentioned in **Gen. 4:17** is that of building a city. Disregard the fact that Cain married his sister (who else could she be) and focus on the parallel lines of Cain and Seth because that's where the real story is. The seventh man from Adam in Cain's line was Lamech, whose name comes from a root meaning "despairing." He had three sons; Jabal a livestock breeder, Jubal a musician, Tubal-cain a toolmaker, and a daughter Naamah. We're not given Naamah's vocation, but her name comes from a root meaning pleasure. Maybe she founded "the Oldest Profession." From these children came animal husbandry, manufacturing, the arts and music, and entertainment. In just 7 generations we see a recognizable civilization; cities in which to live, leisure and entertainment, and industry.

By the way, don't be fooled into thinking of families as they are today with a mom and dad and two kids. These people had 800-year life spans. If on average they only bore children during 200 of these years and only had one every 5 years they would have died with over 2 million descendants each. Multiply that by just the number of people the Bible names and you have a huge population. Remember, they were told to be fruitful and fill the earth (**Gen. 1:28**).

I'm convinced this early civilization was the result of Cain's efforts to find a way around the curse the Lord had pronounced on him. Since the ground would no longer yield crops for him, he and his descendants turned to livestock for their sustenance, wearing their skins and eating their meat, and banded together in cities for protection.

What's My Line?

Adam lay with his wife again, and she gave birth to a son and named him Seth, saying, "God has granted (appointed) me another child in place of Abel, since Cain killed him (**Gen. 4:25**). This verse takes us back in time to introduce the line of Seth. His name means appointed and he assumed the role of redeemer since Cain and Abel had both been disqualified. The seventh man down Seth's line from Adam was Enoch (**Gen. 5:18**). His name means teaching, and in **Gen 5:24** we read that "Enoch walked with God then he was no more, because God took him away. Three generations later came Noah and the Great Flood; 10 generations from Adam, 1656 years after the creation.

The story of Cain's line is the story of unregenerate man. Exalting himself in defiance of God's commandments (**Gen. 4:23-24**), using God given talents to build an Earth centered civilization in an attempt to glorify himself and defeat God's plan. The line of Seth tells a story of the faithful. Due to man's sin nature (ever notice how cities are always more sinful than rural areas?) Cain's line attracted many converts while Seth's dwindled to a small remnant.

When the Great Flood came all the line of Cain perished along with all the accomplishments of their

Earth centered civilization. From the line of Seth only Noah and his family were found faithful. They were preserved through the flood to begin again and the line of Seth ultimately fulfilled God's promise and brought forth The Redeemer; the Son of God, born of Mary a descendant of Seth's through Noah's son Shem.

What About Enoch?

What we have in the story of Cain and Seth is nothing less than a model of the age of man. At the End of the Age the Great Tribulation will see all humankind judged along spiritual lines. Those who have rejected God's ways in favor of an Earth-centered life (the spiritual line of Cain) will perish as Cain's descendants perished in the Great Flood. A small remnant will be preserved through this judgment to begin again (faithful Israel descended from Seth through Shem).

But another group will be taken by God before the Great Tribulation, just as Enoch was taken by Him before the Flood. That group is the Church, also of the spiritual line of Seth.

One body, as Enoch was one body, charged with teaching the Gospel (Enoch means teaching) and like him commanded to walk with God in an unbelieving world, the Church will be taken by God and spared the Great Tribulation just as Enoch was taken by God and spared the Great Flood. By the way, according to Jewish tradition, Enoch was taken on his birthday, a day later known as Pentecost. Since the Church was also born on Pentecost, it would make the model complete to see us raptured on our birthday, wouldn't it? Time will tell.

Now you know the adult version.

Noah and the Flood Part 1 ...
The X Men

When men began to increase in number on the Earth and daughters were born to them, the sons of God saw that the daughters of men were beautiful and they married any of them they chose. Then the Lord said, "My Spirit will not contend with Man forever for he is mortal. His days will be 120 years." The Nephilim were on the earth in those days - and also afterward - when the sons of God went to the daughters of men and had children by them (**Gen. 6:1-4**).

Take this literally, as we always do, and it's four of the scariest verses in the Bible. The Hebrew phrase translated "sons of God" refers to beings who are direct creations of God, normally angels, and distinguishes the origin of the males in the passage from that of the females. Only two human males are ever described this way; Adam (**Luke 3:38**) and the Lord Jesus. In **Psalm 82:6** the rulers of Israel are called children of the Most High but the context refers to their role as judges of the people, responsible for dispensing both justice and mercy. In **John 1:12** we who have received the Lord into our hearts are given the authority to become children of God. There the notion is that of being born again as a spiritual child of God, a concept amplified in **John 3:3-21**.

The Testimony of Two Witnesses

To make sure we get the point of **Genesis 6:1-4**, the distinction appears twice. The males were direct creations of God while the females were the offspring of human parents. The passage clearly implies that fallen angels somehow took on the form of human males and married human females who bore their children. **2 Peter 2:4** and **Jude 6** mention these fallen angels as having been rounded up and bound in chains awaiting the Judgment Day, and in **1 Cor. 6:3** Paul hinted that the church will judge them for their actions. Their children were called *Nephilim* (*gigantes* in Greek ... origin of our word giant) a Hebrew word that translates "fallen ones" and were destroyed in the flood.

But Nephilim also appeared after the flood as foretold in **Gen 6:4** ("and also afterward"). Returning from their first view of the Promised Land, the 12 spies reported seeing them among the local population (**Numbers 13:33**). This is one reason the Lord instructed the Israelites to wipe out all the people of Caanan (**Deut. 20:16-18**) including their animals before settling down in their new land. Like Nephilim, the Rephaim were also called giants and are mentioned through out the Old Testament. Goliath was from the Rephaim. We would call these people aliens today, being of extra-terrestrial origin.

And now research of documented alien encounters shows a consistent interest in and inspection of the human reproductive system. Are aliens using humans to grow and harvest offspring, creating a super race among us as some have claimed? Does the apparent increase in alien contact signal another return of the Nephilim? In the KJV translation of **Daniel 2:43** there's an obscure reference to someone from the 4th kingdom "mingling themselves with the seed of men" in the last days. Is the antichrist part alien, or in command of alien forces? In **Matt 24:37** the Lord spoke of the Last Days being "as it was in the days of Noah." Think about it.

Back To Genesis

The mixed marriages of **Gen. 6** contaminated the human gene pool. Satan was trying to thwart the plan of God by preventing the birth of a Redeemer, since a direct descendant of Adam was required, a man without sin. Fossil evidence reveals that Satan was also tinkering with animal genetics before the flood since the various strains of dinosaurs and such couldn't have been formed any other way. What little we understand of God's creative capability tells us He wouldn't have made an animal with a body too big for its skeleton, and a brain too small to effectively control it. Nor would He have created birds too heavy to fly or fish that couldn't swim. His creation was perfect and He pronounced it all "very good." Fossils were formed at one time and one time only, during the Great Flood, and were left as evidence of pre flood disobedience. Man sinned, allowing Evil into the world, and God had to destroy His contaminated creation and begin again. It's a dreadful thing to fall into the hands of the Living God (**Hebr. 10:31**).

But Noah Found Grace In The Eyes Of The Lord.

Noah was a righteous man, blameless among the people of his time (**Gen. 6:8-9**). The Hebrew here means perfect in his generations, not sinless. Within the above context it's clear that Noah was chosen for two reasons. First, his genealogy was not contaminated by intermarriage so a direct line to Adam could be preserved, and second, he was faithful. Even in the worst of times the Lord has always preserved a faithful remnant to begin again and Noah, though a sinner like all men, had walked with God all his life.

Genesis 6:5-6 says that every intention of man's mind was evil and God saw no alternative to destroying them all. Having given mankind 10 generations, great teachers like Enoch, a living reminder in Methuselah (the name means his death shall bring) and a 120 year count down (**Gen. 6:3**), in the year Methuselah died the Great Flood came, 1656 years after Adam's creation. And the record shows that not one of the world's inhabitants joined Noah on the Ark. Just like the people of our time, they didn't believe God would ever judge them. Like the man said, "The only thing we learn from history is that we never learn anything from history."

Noah and the Flood Part 2 ...
The Big Boat

God saw how corrupt the earth had become, for all the people on earth had corrupted their ways. So God said to Noah, "I am going to put an end to all people for the earth is filled with violence because of them. I am surely going to destroy both them and the earth. So make yourself an ark out of cypress wood, make rooms in it and coat it with pitch inside and out. This is how you are to build it: the ark is to be 450 feet long, 75 feet wide and 45 feet high. Make a roof for the ark and finish it to within 18 inches of the top. Put a door in the side of the ark and make lower, middle, and upper decks (**Gen. 6:12-16**).

Let's address three of the popular arguments that have been raised by scoffers trying to discredit the notion of a world wide flood through which a human family, together with pairs of every animal variety, were preserved in a big boat.

That's a Big Boat

But was the ark big enough? 450 feet is 1 ½ times the length of a football field. Stood on end, the ark would be about as tall as a 45 story office building. At 75 feet wide each of the ark's three decks contained 33,750 square feet of floor space for a total of 101,250. Since the ark was 4.5 stories tall (45 feet) there was over 1.5 million cubic feet of space under its roof, equivalent to a train with 500 boxcars. If you take every animal, from a mouse to an elephant, and average their size, you'll find that sheep are exactly average. I'm told that shippers allocate about 250 sheep per boxcar when moving them by train. A train with 500 cars would accommodate 125,000 sheep or 62,500 pair.

Zoologists recognize about 18,000 species of animals today, so if Noah went by the same figures he would have needed room for about 18,000 pair of animals or 36,000 total plus 5 more of every "clean" variety and every bird specie (**Gen 7:3**). If the total animal count was about 50,000, it would have taken 40% of the ark's capacity to house them. Even if they used ½ of the ark's total space for food storage, Noah would have had 10,125 square feet left for himself and his family.

I personally believe that the animals were put into some form of hibernation or suspended animation and would have needed very little food, otherwise the job of feeding them and cleaning up after them would have been too much for the 8 humans on board to handle. Also there's no mention of either a birth or death among the animal population during the entire 53 weeks they were on board together.

By the way, ever wonder how Noah knew which animals were "clean?" The same way Cain and Abel knew what to bring as an offering. God told them. The Levitical system began in the Garden not in the wilderness. Moses simply put into writing what God's people had always known.

That's a Lot of Water

"I am going to bring floodwaters on the earth to destroy all life under the heavens, every creature that has the breath of life in it. Everything on earth will perish (**Gen 6:17**). Two of every kind of animal and every kind of creature that moves along the ground will come to you" (**Gen 6:20**). I love the cartoons of Noah running around with butterfly nets trying to catch the animals when in fact, God the Creator of all living things put it into their heads to come to Noah.

In the six hundredth year of Noah's life on the seventh day of the second month - on that day all the springs of the great deep burst forth, and the flood-gates of heaven were opened. And rain fell on the earth 40 days and 40 nights (**Gen. 7:11-12**).

By this we know that there were enormous supplies of water available for the flood. First, the springs of the great deep that up till then had irrigated the earth (**Gen. 2:5-6**) were opened up. And then the floodgates of heaven, a water vapor barrier that had protected earth from harmful ultra-violet rays enabling long life spans (**Gen. 1:7-8**) collapsed. This caused rain, which had not yet fallen on earth (**Gen. 2:5-6** and **Hebr. 11:7**) to fall for 40 days and

40 nights. (Ever wonder how it is that if our bodies' cells regenerate on average every seven years, why we deteriorate with age? These ultra violet rays, from which we were once protected, contaminate the regeneration process and shorten our lives. This condition will be reversed in the millennium (**Isa. 65:20-22**).

But Lord ... You Promised

The waters rose and covered the mountains to a depth of more than 20 feet. Everything that moved on the earth perished - birds, livestock, wild animals, all the creatures that swarm on the earth - and mankind. Everything on dry land that had the breath of life in its nostrils died (**Gen. 7:20-22**).

Beside the inclusive intent of this passage, two factors argue undeniably for a world wide flood: the nature of water and the rainbow. Some of the highest mountains on earth are found in the region and water seeks its own level. If it covered the mountains there it would have to cover them everywhere else in the world as well. There are no natural barriers high enough to contain it. And in **Gen. 9:11-17** the Lord promised never to destroy the world by flooding again and put a rainbow in the sky as a token of this promise. There have been many local and regional floods since Noah's time. If Noah's flood was only local, then God has broken His promise over and over again. Arguments against a universal flood are really attempts to deny God's capacity for judgment. The last folks who tried that all drowned. The next ones will burn (**2 Ptr. 3:3-7**).

Noah and the Flood Part 3 ...
Hidden in Plain Sight

-+===◦⊂===+-

L et's go through the account of Noah and the
flood one more time to pick up some of the
tidbits that make these children's stories so exciting,
and that the Lord often seems to hide in plain sight.

Perfect Pitch

The Ark was coated with pitch both inside and
out (**Gen. 6:14**) which in itself is unusual. Coating on
the outside is done to keep a boat waterproof but
coating on the inside is done to preserve it and insure
a long useful life. Noah only needed the Ark once
and only for a year. Did God want it preserved for
some later use? And then there's the Hebrew word
for pitch. It comes from a root meaning atonement,
forgiveness, or pardon and is translated pitch only
here. What's the hidden clue in this word? Is this a
model of God's grace, by which man is pardoned
through faith, rescuing him from judgment? Was the

Ark a type of Christ? (**See 1 Thes. 1:9-10**)

And what about it's resting place? You and I would have the ark land where it could be used as a dwelling or its materials at least cannibalized for other use. Remember it was a ████ s a small hotel. Why did the Lord have it land ██████ he mountains, make Noah leave it, and the██████ it? I've heard Bible archaeologists complain about the fact that no matter what they discover to support the validity of Biblical accounts, people always respond with something like, "That's great. Now if you could just find Noah's Ark." Was the Ark being kept, not for Noah, but for us "upon whom the fulfillment of the ages has come" (**1 Cor. 10:11**) as the final and irrefutable proof of His existence before the next and final judgment?

Bible Archaeology Search and Exploration Institute

Bob Cornuke, founder of BASE Institute, claims that Mt. Sinai is not in Egypt as tradition holds, but in Saudi Arabia. He's been there and stood atop the place called "The Mountain of Moses" in Arabic. Biblical references support his discoveries there and in talking with him I'm convinced he's found the real Mt. Sinai as well as the route the Israelites took to reach it and the place where they crossed the Red Sea. Bob has also climbed Mt. Ararat in Turkey in search of Noah's Ark and wonders if the traditional site for the Ark's location might also be wrong. A literal rendering of **Gen. 11:2** places the mountains of Ararat, mentioned as the Ark's resting place in

Gen. 8:4, somewhere east of ancient Babylon. Other historical sources agree and on a map it looks obvious. Mt. Ararat, so named in modern times, is a volcano several hundred miles north. Perhaps, as Bob and others believe, the Ark is really amidst the Zagros Mountains in Iran, not atop a volcano in Turkey. Hidden in plain sight? Go to www.baseinstitute.org for a copy of his book on the subject.

What Day is This?

And finally there's the date the ark came to rest. The 17th day of the 7th month is recognized in Jewish life to this day, and is even more prominent in Christianity. Here's why. In **Exodus 12:1** the Lord commanded the Israelites to change their calendar. What had been the 7th month ever since the creation was now to become the 1st. We know this because they retained the original calendar and superimposed the new one over it. On the religious calendar (the new one) Passover, which falls in spring, is always the 14th day of the 1st month as commanded in **Exodus 12**, and on the civil calendar (the old one) New Year's Day comes in the fall 6 months later. So with this 6 month offset what in Noah's day had been the 7th month became the 1st month of the new religious calendar.

On the 17th day of that month the Ark ran aground and for the first time Noah and his family knew from experience that their new life had begun. According to Sir Robert Anderson and the London Royal Observatory, a study of the lunar cycle through the centuries shows that it was a Sunday.

In Judaism the Feast of First Fruits is celebrated on the Sunday that follows Passover (**Lev 23:9-11**) so each time Passover (the 14th) falls on a Thursday the Feast of First Fruits is the 17th three days later. Noah and his family were the first fruits of the New World; a world born again.

2000 years later on that same date, also a Sunday and the Feast of First Fruits, a sealed tomb in Jerusalem was found open and empty. The Lord had been raised from the dead, the First Fruits of those who have fallen asleep (**1 Cor 15:20**). For followers of Jesus the 17th day of the 1st month was Resurrection Morning and for the first time the disciples knew from experience that their new life had begun. That evening they received the Holy Spirit; men born again (**John 20:19-22**).

Just as the Ark had preserved faithful Noah's family through the past judgment and became a model of God's Grace, The Lord Jesus will preserve faithful Israel through the coming judgment, the Personification of Grace. Just as Noah was cast adrift in a world under judgment and experienced the grounding that signified a world born again, a seeker cast adrift in a life under judgment today looks to the cross and the empty tomb and experiences the "grounding" that signifies a life born again.

Now you know the adult version.

The Tower of Babel

Now the whole earth was of one language and of one speech. And it came to pass as they journeyed from the east that they found a plain in the land of Shinar and they dwelt there (**Gen. 11:1-2**).

The story of the Tower of Babel begins in **Genesis 11** but gives us the reason for the formation of the 70 prime nations or ethnic groupings outlined in **Genesis 10**. The Lord had told Noah and his family to "be fruitful and increase in number and fill the earth (**Gen. 9: 1**). But Noah's descendants had decided to remain on the plains of Shinar and build a civilization for themselves there, following the pattern of the Cainites before the Flood (See Cain and Seth). They determined to "build ourselves a city with a tower that reaches to the heavens so that we may make a name for ourselves and not be scattered over the face of the earth (**Gen. 11:4**). This was contrary to God's instructions of course and guaranteed to cause problems.

Where Are We?

Here's something I find interesting. They settled on the plains of Shinar an area we know as Mesopotamia, modern Iraq. They had come from the east, or Iran, where the ark had settled. Beneath this area today lies some of the world's largest known oil reserves. Oil comes from the decomposition of vegetation, and the Tigris and Euphrates rivers that border the area (Mesopotamia means between the rivers) are mentioned in the Creation account as flowing through the Garden of Eden. When it came to building materials for their city and tower, the people chose tar as a substitute for mortar, there being no cement handy. Put all this circumstantial evidence together and you can surmise that the Garden of Eden encompassed the whole region, and was buried under tons and tons of sand after the flood. The weight of the sand compressed the decaying vegetation and helped produce the oil that then bubbled up out of the ground as tar. But that's a story for another day.

Back To Babel

But the Lord came down to see the city and the tower the men were building (**Gen. 11:6**). Enough of the ruins of the Tower of Babel have been discovered to permit archaeologists to speculate on its appearance and purpose. It covered 4 acres at its base and was 153 feet tall. There were 7 stages, each one smaller than the one below, giving it the appearance of a gigantic wedding cake. Each stage was dedicated to one of the then known planets, and a tower at the top had the 12 signs of the zodiac inscribed in the walls. It was apparently intended as a combination observatory and temple to enable the people to worship the celestial bodies and practice astrology.

What Sign Are You?

The 12 signs of the zodiac are a perversion of the Hebrew Mazzaroth. By tradition Adam, Seth, and Enoch named 12 constellations of the stars in such a way as to foretell the gospel story. As shepherds lay under the stars at night fathers could use them to instruct their sons on the Lord's plan of redemption for His fallen people (Read "The Gospel in the Stars" by J.A. Seiss). The "horror-scope" in your newspaper lists the Babylonian names of these constellations. In reading it you are inadvertently following the false religion that originated with the tower of Babel and that denies everything the Bible says about the relationship that began with your Creator at the moment of conception. These corrupt names are virtually the same in every known language except Hebrew where the true names and meanings of the 12 signs can be learned. This is why the study of astrology (observer of times KJV) was an offense punishable by death in Israel and was given as one of the causes for the Canaanites' expulsion from the Promised Land (**Deut. 18:9-11**).

Justice and Mercy

Come, let us go down and confuse their language so they will not understand each other. So the Lord scattered them from there all over the earth and they stopped building the City. That is why it was called Babel - because the Lord confused the language of the whole world (**Gen. 11:7-9**).

Once again an act of judgment contained an element of mercy. By stopping things when He did the Lord prevented the people from going entirely astray and bringing about their complete destruction. Confusing their language curtailed their misplaced spirit of cooperation and so they separated, accomplished God's purpose, and escaped a much greater penalty. Hidden in every human effort to unite in common cause you'll find Satan's strategy of separating us from our Creator. If achieving God's will is not the overriding issue whether in a group of individuals or a community of nations, Satan orchestrates our utter defeat by simply appealing to our sense of pride and self-determination.

Are We Related?

I believe God first separated the people by physical appearance based on their family lines. The children of Ham became the Egyptian and other African races, those of Shem became the Arabs and Jews, and those of Japeth became the Chinese, Russian and European peoples. Within a generation or two inbreeding caused the dominant and recessive genetic patterns of each group to make them even more easily distinguishable from one another. Language differences completed the separation into the 70 nations listed in Genesis 10, and for a time sinful man's natural inclination to rebel against God was thwarted.

Now you know the adult version.

Sodom and Gomorrah

One day while Abraham was sitting outside his campsite, he looked up and saw three visitors approaching. Following the custom of the day, Abraham offered them refreshment and rest from their journey. When he discovered it was the Lord and two angels, he had Sarah quickly make some unleavened bread, milk and curds, and had a servant slaughter and prepare a young calf.

After their meal the Lord announced that the time had come for His 20 year old promise of a child for Abraham and Sarah to be fulfilled. Sarah overheard them talking and laughed to herself. She was 90 years old after all. The Lord had heard her laugh in her heart before and told them they should name the child Isaac, which means laughter.

As they were leaving, the Lord decided to let Abraham in on the real purpose of His visit. "The outcry against Sodom and Gomorrah is so great and their sin so grievous that I will go down there to see if what they have done is as bad as the outcry that has reached me. If not I will know." (**Gen. 18:20-21**)

During the brief negotiating session that followed this news, Abraham convinced the Lord that if even 10 righteous people could be found in the cities, the Lord would spare them. Perhaps Abraham was thinking about his nephew Lot, who lived there with his wife and two daughters.

The two angels came to Sodom and asked for directions to the central square, where they planned to spend the night. It happened that they inquired of Lot, who insisted they spend the night at his home instead.

After dinner some of the men of the city, having had too much to drink, came to Lot's house and demanded he turn over his visitors so they could have sex with them. Lot refused. The custom of the day required that Lot defend his guests with his life if necessary. He even offered the men his two daughters rather than turn over his guests, but they refused and became even more belligerent.

Just as Lot was about to be overpowered, the two angels struck the men blind and since in their confusion they could no longer find the door to his house, the crowd dispersed.

Get Outa Town

The angels then told Lot to gather up his family and leave quickly because they were going to destroy the whole area. Lot rounded up his family, but the two young men betrothed to his daughters refused to leave. The angels grabbed Lot, his wife and daughters and hustled them out of the city, telling them to hurry and not look back because they couldn't do anything until the family was safe. But Lot's wife could not resist one last look and as she turned, the force of the destruction over took her and her body was crystallized into a pillar of salt.

Early the next day as Abraham looked down the road toward Sodom he saw the cloud of smoke from its destruction rising in the morning sky, and knew the cities had been destroyed. But God had remembered His promise to Abraham and had spared Lot and his daughters.

Sodom ... Home Of The Alternative Lifestyle

The city of Sodom gave its name to a form of sexual behavior traditionally practiced by male homosexuals. So given over to this behavior were the men of Sodom that they refused to entertain themselves with Lot's virgin daughters instead of the two angels, even though Lot's offer was sincere.

There must have been behavior in Sodom even more displeasing to the Lord than what they exhibited that night because in **Romans 1:21-27** Paul explained that homosexuality comes as an outcome of denying our Lord, exchanging the worship of Him for the worship of created things instead. This is not ignorance, understand, but disobedience. Having known Him they've rejected Him. Homosexuality is described as a result of the rejection. And don't forget. The women of Sodom were judged as well.

Everybody's Doing It ... Aren't They?

Through out history homosexuality has become an accepted, even encouraged, practice in nearly every civilization in the advanced stages of its decline. As we in the USA journey further into what's been called our "post-Christian" era we can expect to see more of it. This in spite of the fact that over 2 out of every 3 Americans describe themselves as Christian. But the Lord looks more at what we do than what we say, and still more at what we think than what we do. The spread of homosexuality is one level of indication of our decline, our tolerance and acceptance of it is quite another. As Billy Graham said a few years back, "If God doesn't judge the USA, He'll have to apologize to Sodom and Gomorrah."

The story of Sodom and Gomorrah denies the notion of genetic pre-disposition toward homosexuality. If it was a hereditary trait the Lord couldn't have judged them for it any more than He could have judged them for having blue eyes. Yet in **Leviticus 18:22** he forbade it, calling it detestable. Forbidding it implies we can keep ourselves from it. God is just after all.

Sure, I think at some level every human being has some potential for homosexuality, and a surprising number of people admit to having experimented with it. We also all have the potential for alcoholism and a whole myriad of other crimes and addictions. We're sinners, after all. The potential for sin is part of our nature. It's a disease of the blood and on Earth there's no cure, but the Lord provided an antidote.

Confession and Forgiveness. It'll keep us alive until He administers the transfusion that finally cures us forever.

What're We Going To Do About It?

"Hate the sin, love the sinner," we're told. Instead some of us love (accept) the sin, while others hate (reject) the sinner. In that sense the homophobes who parade with their signs, "God hates fags" are not only wrong (He loves us all) but are sinning as surely as the folks they're demonstrating against.

No one will voluntarily turn to a God they who they think hates them, but rather to quote Paul again, "It's His kindness that leads us to repentance." (**Rom 2:4**) And likewise no one will feel the need to confess and receive forgiveness for something that they think many around them consider only an "alternative lifestyle."

Somehow a homosexual needs to feel free to come to the Lord "just as I am" like every other kind of sinner can and receive the forgiveness the Lord purchased for all of us with His own blood. At that point the behavior is between the two of them, and can best be resolved privately.

We're all sinners in need of a savior, and all sin leads to judgment and death. The failure that brought judgment on the people of Sodom and Gomorrah was not their particular sexual sin. It was their rejection of God and the remedy He offered them.

Now you know the adult version.

Abraham and Isaac
(the Gospel in Genesis)

S ome time later God tested Abraham. He said to him, "Abraham!" "Here I am," he replied. Then God said, "Take your son, your only son Isaac, whom you love, and go to the region of Moriah. Sacrifice him there as a burnt offering on one of the mountains I will tell you about" (**Genesis 22:1-2**)

This is perhaps the most misunderstood of all the children's stories, but the clues that will lead us to a correct understanding are hidden in plain sight right in the passage. Some interpretations of this story would have us believe that God is so insecure as to force us to make such an agonizing choice as the one with which He confronted Abraham, just to prove we really love him. Is that the case, or was there more going on than meets the eye? Let's find out.

The first clue is in God's use of Abraham's covenant name. This tells us that He had already agreed to bless and protect Abraham, and make him the father of many nations. The covenant was unilateral and required no commitment from Abraham to remain in force. (He had put Abraham to sleep during the ceremony.) Also by calling Isaac Abraham's only son it's clear God didn't think Isaac expendable in the matter, that He intended Isaac as the child of the promise. Surely Ishmael, Abraham's firstborn would also be blessed, but it was through Isaac that the covenant would be actualized (**Gen. 17:19-22**). Already an interesting parallel is emerging between what God was asking Abraham to do and what He would later do Himself.

Your Only Beloved Son

In **John 3:16** Jesus is called God's only son, but is he? **Luke 3:37-38** refers to Adam as the son of God. Adam preceded Jesus in birth order, but Jesus occupies the ceremonial position of firstborn, inheriting all its rights and privileges. He is always referred to as the only Son of God. Ishmael was born to Abraham and Hagar 19 years before Sarah gave birth to Isaac, and according to human law was the legitimate firstborn, but God didn't recognize him as such. Isaac is called Abraham's only son.

And then there's the location; the region of Moriah. Mt. Moriah is the place where Solomon later built the temple (**2 Chron. 3:1**). Just north of the Temple area Jesus would be sacrificed as an offering for the sins of the world, on the same spot where Abraham was being asked to offer Isaac. Be sure to notice that God didn't say He would show Abraham the place but would tell him about it, probably during the 3 days it took for Abraham and Isaac to get there.

Three Days And Three Nights
On the third day Abraham looked up and saw the place in the distance. He said to his servants, "Stay here with the donkey while I and the boy go over there. We will worship and then we will come back to you". Abraham took the wood for the burnt offering and placed it on his son Isaac, and he himself carried the fire and the knife (**Gen. 22:4-6**). Did God really intend for Abraham to bind Isaac, slit his throat, place him upon the altar and burn him there? In **Deut. 18:9-13** God expressly forbade such an act. Would He ask Abraham to do something against His own law? As the two of them went on together Isaac spoke up and said to his father Abraham, "Father?" "Yes my son," Abraham replied. "The fire and the wood are here but where is the lamb for the burnt offering?" Abraham answered, "God himself will provide the lamb for the burnt offering, my son." And the two of them went on together (**Gen. 22:6-8**).

Grace Through Faith
Hebrews 11:17-19 explains that Abraham did this by faith, knowing all along that God, who cannot lie, had promised him a long line of descendants through Isaac, and yet at this time Isaac had no children. He *reasoned* that God could raise the dead, and figuratively speaking he did receive Isaac back from the death. This was not just an act of blind faith. Being in a covenant relationship with God and

knowing His nature and character, Abraham trusted God, placing the outcome in His hands. I believe that along the way God revealed the details to Abraham enabling him to tell the servants that "we will worship and then we will come back to you" and to tell Isaac that "God himself will provide the lamb for the burnt offering." The Lord subsequently did this (**Gen. 22:13**) and the innocent ram God provided died in Isaac's place.

It fascinates me that this entire drama unfolded over 3 days and 3 nights. By the way, the word that's translated boy in v.6 means a young man of military age (18-30), and in v.8 the word for together means united and comes from a root meaning to become as one. Apparently Isaac was an adult in on the plan all along and participating by agreement.

Shades Of The Everlasting Covenant

Based on these clues, it seems clear that Abraham and Isaac were acting out a prophecy wherein another Father would later give His only Son as an offering for sin on the very same spot. As with Abraham and Isaac, this Father and Son would be doing so by prior agreement, in this case one made before the foundation of the world was laid. And as God provided an innocent ram to die in place of Isaac, so He would provide the innocent Lamb of God, Who would die in our place. It makes sense then that Abraham named the location "Jehovah Jireh" meaning on the mountain of the Lord it will be provided. Because it was. On that very place.

Now you know the adult version.

Isaac and Rebecca
(The Gospel in Genesis ...
Part 2)

❖══◉══❖

T hen Abraham returned to his servants and they
set off together for Beersheba. And Abraham
stayed in Beersheba (**Gen. 22:19**). Students have
puzzled over this verse. Abraham had told his
servants that he and Isaac would return to them (v.5),
and the Lord had provided a substitute offering sparing Isaac (v.13) so why doesn't the verse read
"Abraham and Isaac returned to their servants ... "?
The answer is hidden in plain sight in chapter 24
when Isaac re-appears and completes the story of the
Gospel in Genesis.

In **Gen. 24:1** we read that Abraham was now old
and well advanced in years and the Lord had blessed
him in every way. Sarah had died and Abraham had
buried her in Hebron (**Gen. 23**) so he sent the chief
servant in his household to the home of his relatives

to choose a wife for Isaac, traditionally a mother's privilege. Abraham instructed him that he was not to get Isaac a bride from the Canaanites, nor was he to take Isaac back to his homeland. If the woman he chose refused to come, then the servant was released from his duty (**Gen. 24:1-9**).

Will You Marry Him?

The servant packed 10 camels with gifts and set out for the town where Nahor, Abraham's brother, lived. On the way he devised a plan that he asked the Lord to bless as he was arriving at the well outside town. The deal was that if he asked a girl for a drink and she offered to help water his camels as well, she would be the one the Lord had selected for Isaac. Now drawing enough water for 10 camels is no small task so this would be a real sign. Before he had finished praying, Rebekah came along and when he asked her for a drink she agreed and offered to water his camels as well. The servant confirmed that she was from the family of Nahor (she was his granddaughter) gave her gifts, and asked to spend the night with the family.

Upon arriving at her family home, the servant told his story and formally asked for Rebekah on behalf of Isaac. They gave their permission but when the servant insisted that they leave immediately said the final decision was hers. With out hesitation she agreed to go and they set off (**Gen. 24:10-61**).

Isaac had come in from the desert to Beer Lahai Roi one evening and as he looked up in the distance he saw them coming and went out to meet them.

Rebekah spotted him and asked the servant who he was. "He is my master," the servant replied so she covered herself with a veil as was the custom. Isaac brought her into the tent of his mother Sarah and married her and she brought comfort to Isaac after his mother's death. (**Gen. 24:62-67**)

The Well Of Living Water

This is about as good a model of the relationship between the Father, the Son, Israel, and the Church as you'll find anywhere in scripture. Remember that from the command to offer his only son as a sacrifice, Isaac was as good as dead to Abraham. Three days later Abraham received Isaac back from death when the Lord provided a substitute sacrifice (**Gen. 22:4-6, 13 & Hebr. 11:17-19**). At this point Isaac disappeared from the story. Abraham returned home with the servants to preside over the death and burial of his beloved Sarah and send an unnamed servant to the land of his family to obtain a bride for Isaac. She is supernaturally identified to the servant, given gifts by him, and must decide immediately to leave her familiar life, embark upon a journey of unknown duration with the servant as her guide to marry a husband she has never seen. Isaac is re-introduced into the story on the occasion of their initial meeting (on a day and hour previously unknown to her) near Beer LaHai Roi where they finally meet face to face and are married. Roughly translated Beer LaHai Roi means well of living water.

I Spoke To The Prophets, Gave Them Many Visions, And Told Parables Through Them (Hosea 12:10)

After God the Father had received His Son back from death, Jesus ascended into heaven and disappeared from Earth. Later the Father presided over the death and burial of His beloved Israel. He also sent an unnamed Servant into the Earth in search of a bride for His Son. This Servant, The Holy Spirit, is called The Comforter by Jesus in **John 16:7 KJV** but is known by no other name. (Although Abraham's servant is not named in **Gen. 24**, a few chapters earlier he is identified as Eliezer a name that roughly translates "God is our comforter" **Gen.15:2**).

The Holy Spirit seeks out supernaturally identified people (He knew us before the foundation of the Earth was laid) asking us to become the Bride of Christ, investing us with gifts when we agree (**Ephe. 1:13-14** and **1Cor. 12:7-11**). We must decide immediately to leave our familiar life, and embark upon a spiritual journey of unknown duration with the Comforter as our guide to marry a husband we have never seen. On a day and hour previously unknown to us our Bethrothed will come out to meet us (**1 Thes. 4:16-17**), The Holy Spirit will usher us into the presence of the true Well of Living Water, and upon meeting Him face to face for the first time we will wed.

Now you know the adult version.

Jacob and Esau

Abraham's son Isaac had married Rebekah, and though they wanted children, Rebekah was unable to conceive. Isaac prayed to the Lord and she became pregnant … with twins!

The babies jostled each other within her, and she said, "Why is this happening to me?" So she went to inquire of the Lord. The Lord said to her,

> "Two nations are in your womb,
> and two peoples from within you will be separated;
> one people will be stronger than the other,
> and the older will serve the younger."

When the time came for her to give birth, there were twin boys in her womb. The first to come out was red, and his whole body was like a hairy garment; so they named him Esau. After this, his brother came out, with his hand grasping Esau's heel; so he was named Jacob. Isaac was sixty years old when Rebekah gave birth to them.

The boys grew up, and Esau became a skillful hunter, a man of the open country, while Jacob was a quiet man, staying among the tents. Isaac, who had a taste for wild game, loved Esau, but Rebekah loved Jacob.

Once when Jacob was cooking some stew, Esau came in from the open country, hungry. He said to Jacob, "Quick, let me have some of that red stew! I'm famished!" (That is why he was also called Edom.)

Jacob replied, "First sell me your birthright."

"Look, I am about to die," Esau said. "What good is the birthright to me?"

But Jacob said, "Swear to me first." So he swore an oath to him, selling his birthright to Jacob.

Then Jacob gave Esau some bread and some lentil stew. He ate and drank, and then got up and left.

So Esau despised his birthright. (**Gen 25:22-34**)

Born Contenders

These brothers were contentious from the beginning. Esau, which means hairy, was born a few minutes before Jacob, his name meaning conniver or schemer. Easu was also called Edom, or red, from the color of the lentil stew he traded his birthright for. That's the name he gave to his descendants, who settled the area north east of the Dead Sea in today's Jordan. The Herods, who ruled over Israel in Roman times were from Edom.

Esau and Jacob belong to the series of sons born

to the patriarchs whose lives showcase the Lord's ability to regain with a younger son losses incurred by the firstborn; losses that could have damaged or even destroyed man's hope for redemption. It's a model of man's second chance.

The Firstborn

A firstborn son had special rights and responsibilities. He was the official kinsman redeemer, responsible for preserving the family's assets by buying back what a brother had lost or mortgaged (or purchasing his freedom in cases of debt that led to slavery). He was also the avenger of blood. Since there was no organized police force in those days, the firstborn was responsible for seeing that those who caused the shedding of family blood paid their just penalty. Eye for eye, tooth for tooth, limb for limb and life for life. He served as head of the family in the absence of his father. It was such an important position that his reward for assuming this responsibility was a double share of his father's estate.

Lost By One, Regained By The Other

But for one reason or another several firstborn sons either lost or gave up their position in favor of a younger one. Think of Cain and Seth, where Seth re-established the connection to mankind's redeemer broken by Cain's murder of Abel. Or Ishmael and Isaac, where Isaac remained the supernaturally born son of the promise even though Abraham and Sarah jumped the gun by appointing a surrogate mother to birth Ishmael. And Esau thought so little of his position as firstborn that he sold it to Jacob for a bowl of stew and earned the Lord's condemnation.

"Was not Esau Jacob's brother?" the LORD says. "Yet I have loved Jacob, but Esau I have hated, and I have turned his mountains into a wasteland and left his inheritance to the desert jackals." Edom may say, "Though we have been crushed, we will rebuild the ruins." But this is what the LORD Almighty says: "They may build, but I will demolish. They will be called the Wicked Land, a people always under the wrath of the LORD. You will see it with your own eyes and say, 'Great is the LORD -even beyond the borders of Israel!' (**Mal 1:2-5**)

In fact Jacob became so much more prominent than his brother that the order of names has been reversed in referring to them, just as God had told Rebekah before their birth. The contention between them never really went away, and as Moses was leading the Israelites up the King's Highway from Egypt toward Jericho several hundred years later, the Edomites refused them any water even though Moses offered to pay for it. Much later, under King David, Israel conquered Edom completing the fulfillment of the Lord's prophecy to Rebekah. And today, while Israel is once again center stage in the world, Edom long ago ceased to exist as a people.

Of course the ultimate case to which all these sons point is Adam, the first son of God (**Luke 3:38**) who lost planet Earth and all his descendants, and Jesus Who regained it all and more (**Rom. 5:12-19**).

Our Kinsman Redeemer

Jesus came to Earth with obligations as both Kinsman Redeemer and Avenger of Blood and had to be all God and all Man to fulfill them. To regain the property Adam had lost, He had to buy it back. To redeem Adam's progeny from their bondage of sin He had to pay off our debts. This was the responsibility of the Kinsman Redeemer and the required currency for both transactions was the blood of a sinless man.

As the Avenger of Blood, he had to bring Adam and Eve's murderer to justice. Remember, they were immortal until they sinned. When Satan disputed God's warning that eating the forbidden fruit would cause their deaths, he was lying. By persuading them to disobey God, Satan orchestrated their demise and was responsible for their deaths. Only someone with all the authority and power of God could subdue such a powerful adversary.

Our Lord Jesus did all of this at the cross. He paid all our debts.

When you were dead in your sins and in the uncircumcision of your sinful nature, God made you alive with Christ. He forgave us all our sins, having canceled the written code, with its regulations, that was against us and that stood opposed to us; he took it away, nailing it to the cross. And having disarmed the powers and authorities, he made a public spectacle of them, triumphing over them by the cross. **(Colossians 2:13-15)**

Turning what Satan believed was his greatest

victory into his total defeat, Jesus made a public spectacle of him. By His one act of sacrifice He purchased a complete pardon for all who would accept it, releasing them forever from the bondage of sin. Since that time he waits for his enemies to be made his footstool, because by one sacrifice he has made perfect forever those who are being made holy. **(Hebr. 10:13-14)**

He also redeemed Planet Earth.

The creation waits in eager expectation for the sons of God to be revealed. For the creation was subjected to frustration, not by its own choice, but by the will of the one who subjected it, in hope that the creation itself will be liberated from its bondage to decay and brought into the glorious freedom of the children of God. **(Rom. 8:19-21)**

And He sealed Satan's destiny of defeat in the spiritual realm. We await only the signal from God that the time has come, to witness his capture and death in the physical one.

Those who see you stare at you, they ponder your fate: "Is this the man who shook the earth and made kingdoms tremble, the man who made the world a desert, who overthrew its cities and would not let his captives go home?"

All the kings of the nations lie in state, each in his own tomb. But you are cast out of your tomb like a rejected branch; you are covered with the slain, with those pierced by the sword, those who descend to the stones of the pit. Like a corpse trampled underfoot, you will not join them in burial, for you have destroyed your land and killed your people. **(Isaiah 14:16-20)**

And the devil, who deceived them, was thrown into the lake of burning sulfur, where the beast and the false prophet had been thrown. They will be tormented day and night forever and ever. **(Rev. 20:10)**

Now you know the adult version.

Jacob's Ladder

Jacob left Beersheba and set out for Haran. When he reached a certain place, he stopped for the night because the sun had set. Taking one of the stones there, he put it under his head and lay down to sleep. He had a dream in which he saw a stairway resting on the earth, with its top reaching to heaven, and the angels of God were ascending and descending on it. There above it stood the LORD, and he said: "I am the LORD, the God of your father Abraham and the God of Isaac. I will give you and your descendants the land on which you are lying. Your descendants will be like the dust of the earth, and you will spread out to the west and to the east, to the north and to the south. All peoples on earth will be blessed through you and your offspring. I am with you and will watch over you wherever you go, and I will bring you back to this land. I will not leave you until I have done what I have promised you."

When Jacob awoke from his sleep, he thought,

"Surely the LORD is in this place, and I was not aware of it." He was afraid and said, "How awesome is this place! This is none other than the house of God; this is the gate of heaven." **(Genesis 28:12-17)**

How Do You Explain That?

Jacob, his name means conniver, had just tricked Isaac into giving him the blessing his twin brother Esau thought he should have had. Esau swore to kill him, so their mother warned Jacob to flee to her family's home in Paddan Aram, some distance away. "When your brother calms down," she told him. I'll send for you." **(Gen. 27:44-45)**

He was a little north of the place that would become Jerusalem near Shiloh, where the tabernacle stood when the Israelites first came into the Promised Land and where a growing number of scholars today believe the Millennial Temple will stand. As Jacob dreamt of the stairway leading from Earth into Heaven the Lord spoke to him, renewing the covenant He had made with Abraham **(Gen. 15)** and then Isaac **(Gen. 17:19)**.

In each case it was clear. The covenant was unconditional: a free gift to Abraham's descendants. Abraham had neither asked for it, nor was any compensation ever mentioned (although Joshua learned that to actually occupy the land, the Israelites would have to dispossess the indigenous residents.)

The locals were a 10 nation confederacy of pagan tribes the Lord had earlier given 400 years to repent of their idolatry and return to Him. Since they had ignored His warnings, He brought the Israelites to act as His agency of judgment against them. And just so the Israelites would know the outcome was never in doubt, the Lord went before them to frighten and weaken their enemies, stopping the Jordan's flow, tearing down their walls and even making the Sun and Moon stand still in the sky. In fact the only casualties the Bible records in the whole campaign came from the battle of Ai, where the Israelites were disobedient to God and thereby deprived of His help.

We're A Little Ahead Of Our Time

But this was all still several centuries in the future when the Lord spoke to Jacob in his dream. What Jacob knew was that he stood on Holy Ground. As he prepared to continue on his journey, he named the place Bethel, which means "House of God."

Nearly 20 centuries later Jesus, recalling Jacob's dream, identified Himself as the stairway on which the angels of God were ascending and descending. (**John 2:51**) In so doing He declared that He was a kind of vertical bridge between Heaven and Earth, spanning the awful chasm between them caused by sin's entry into the world.

But Wait, There's More

And not only that. Just as He explained that the stairway was symbolic of Him, so did He show that the place Jacob had named Bethel was symbolic of the nation Israel. For though Bethel is indeed located in the Promised Land, it's really the descendants of Jacob who are the "House of God." They are His people, and it was through them that the Messiah Redeemer had come to be our Stairway to Heaven. For in the bargain God opened His house to the Gentiles as well. (**Gal. 3:26-29**)

Because of his dream, Jacob thought he had stumbled onto some mysterious portal to another world, the "Gate of Heaven." But later Jesus would claim that the gate stood for Him as well. "I am the gate: whoever enters through Me will be saved." (**John 10:9**)

Heaven and Earth were once unified and the only will was God's will. Then sin entered the world through Satan's great deception and with it came man's loss of immortality. Access to the Garden was forbidden, but an angel was stationed at its entrance, "guarding the way to the Tree of Life" signifying that one day man would again become immortal.

But first that awful chasm that had separated man from God would have to be bridged. The Lord chose the Jewish people to be His own and through them brought forth the Messiah to accomplish just that. With His shed blood the Messiah built a stairway to Heaven, and with His death became the gate. All who enter through Him (believing His death purchased a pardon for their sins) whether Jew or Gentile would become immortal, climb the Stairway to Heaven and dwell in the House of God forever.

Now you know the adult version.

Joseph and His Coat
of Many Colors

Joseph, a young man of seventeen. was tending the flocks with his brothers, the sons of Bilhah and the sons of Zilpah, his father's wives, and he brought their father a bad report about them. Now Israel (Jacob) loved Joseph more than any of his other sons because he had been born to him in his old age; and he made a richly ornamented robe for him. When his brothers saw that their father loved him more than any of them, they hated him and could not speak a kind word to him (**Gen. 37:2-4**).

You know the story. Joseph had two dreams. In one he and his 11 brothers were represented by sheaves of wheat. During the dream their sheaves all bowed down before his. In the other the sun, moon and 11 stars were all bowing before him. Jacob interpreted this to mean that these celestial bodies represented him, Joseph's mother, and the 11 brothers. This further incensed them making their rejection complete. One day when Jacob had sent Joseph to find his brothers and inquire about their well being they conspired against him, captured him and threw him into a pit. Then they sold him to slave traders bound for Egypt. They faked his death, showing their father his fancy robe all covered in blood as evidence of Joseph's untimely demise. As far as Jacob was concerned, his beloved son was dead.

You Can't Keep A Good Man Down

Arriving in Egypt, Joseph was purchased by Potiphar, the captain of Pharoah's guard, and quickly rose to a position of trust in his household. Angered because Joseph refused her sexual advances, Potiphar's wife had him thrown into jail on false charges. Again he rose to a prominent position, overseeing the entire prison operation. While there he interpreted the dreams of two prisoners and when his interpretations proved correct he was called to the attention of Pharoah, who had also had a disturbing dream. Joseph interpreted this dream as a prediction of 7 good harvest years to be followed by 7 years of famine so severe they would wipe out all the gains of the good years and then some.

Pharoah appointed Joseph, a man without station or influence, to devise a strategy to save the people from this famine and made him the number 2 authority in all Egypt subject only to Pharoah. During the good years Joseph married the daughter of an Egyptian priest and by successfully implementing his strategy when the famine came, Joseph saved them all from certain death, enabling Pharoah to take possession of Egypt and all its wealth in the process.

What They Intended For Evil, God Intended For Good

When the famine reached the land of Caanan, Jacob sent his sons to Egypt to purchase food. Not recognizing the one from whom they were buying as their long lost brother, these 11 were put through a series of disastrous events contrived by Joseph to place them entirely at his mercy and permit the revelation of his true identity. A highly emotional reunion resulted in Jacob and the 70 members of his family being given the most favored land in all of Egypt. By the way, Joseph's dreams did come true. Jacob and his wives, and the 11 brothers and their wives and all their children bowed down before Joseph, who had saved them all and brought them into a land of plenty where they enjoyed generations of peace and prosperity.

I Spoke To The Prophets, Gave Them Many Visions, And Told Parables Through Them (Hosea 12:10)

Parables are heavenly truths put into earthly context and the Bible abounds with them. The ones Jesus told are mostly stories He devised for the purpose, but the Lord told Paul that He often orchestrated real life events in Israel to help teach us about Him (**Rom 15:4 & 1 Cor: 10:11**). In this story Jacob and his family represent Israel, Joseph the Messiah, and Pharoah God the Father. Joseph's gentile bride is the church and Egypt the world. The seven good years are the Age of Grace during which the Gentile Bride is taken, the 7 bad years the Tribulation period where the Messiah is revealed to Israel. The land of Goshen is the Kingdom Age. Put the Heavenly Players in place of the earthly ones to gain the lesson and see the Old Testament come alive as never before.

Tell Me A Story, Daddy

Although our Lord Jesus was sent to His brothers to see to their well being, they rejected Him, conspiring against Him and causing His death. He was consigned to Hell, sold as a slave to sin. He had no earthly station or influence but was appointed by God to save the world from sin. He was given a position of prominence on earth receiving all power and authority subject only to the will of God. By successfully implementing His strategy He saved us all from certain death, enabling God to regain possession of the world and all its wealth in the process. After taking a Gentile Bride He will put His brothers through a series of disastrous events contrived to place them entirely at His mercy and permit the revelation of His true identity. A highly emotional reunion will result in Israel again receiving the most favored land in all the Earth where they will enjoy 1000 years of peace and prosperity

We've just scratched the surface here; there are over 100 clear truths being modeled in the life of Joseph. The rest is up to you.

Now you know the adult version.

Moses ...
The Prince of Egypt

As the sun was setting Abram fell into a deep sleep and a thick and dreadful darkness came over him. Then the Lord said to him, "Know for certain that your descendants will be strangers in a country not their own and they will be enslaved and mistreated 400 years. But I will punish the nation they serve as slaves and afterward they will come out with great possessions. You however will go to your fathers in peace and be buried at a good old age. In the 4th generation your descendants will come back here for the sin of the Amorites has not yet reached its full measure. On that day the Lord made a covenant with Abram and said, "To your descendants I give this land from the River of Egypt (Wadi al Arish) to the great river, the Euphrates – the land of the Kenites, Kenizzites, Kadmonites,

Hittites, Perizites, Rephaites, Amorites, Canaanites, Girgashites, and Jebusites. (**Gen. 15:12-16, 18-21**).

As the story of Joseph ended, the family of Israel had been relocated into Egypt and given its finest land in return for the incredible services Joseph had performed in saving all Egypt, while vastly enriching Pharoah. So how did Egypt's honored guests become despised slaves by the time Moses was born?

What Have You Done For Me Lately?

The explanation, **Exodus 1:8-22,** was summarized by Stephen as he reviewed Israel's history before the Sanhedrin. "As the time came for God to fulfill his promise to Abraham the number of our people greatly increased. Then another king, who knew nothing about Joseph, became ruler of Egypt. He dealt treacherously with our people and oppressed our forefathers by forcing them to throw out their newborn babies so that they would die (**Acts 7:17-19**)."

400 years is a long time to remember anything, especially when Egyptian life spans were only about 35 years. Remember this, within one generation the children of Israel had forgotten all about the miracles associated with their arrival in the promised land, even though elaborate attempts were made to help them remember, and it had been one of their greatest victories (**Judges 2:10**). Over 10 Egyptian generations had passed and the family of Israel had become a people numbering in excess of 1 million. They were now a feared and hated minority. There's also an indication from the Greek language of Acts 7

that Egypt's then current ruler was not from the same family as the Pharoah of Joseph's time, and maybe not even Egyptian.

Into this environment Moses was born. By tradition, his mother had a vision that her baby boy would redeem his people. That's why she went to such extremes to protect him from the edict that brought death to all Jewish infant boys. This extended even to floating him down the river to be retrieved by Pharoah's daughter. And so Pharoah provided a home, education, and military training for the one who would ultimately bring about his downfall.

400 Years or 4 Generations, Which is it?

Scoffers note the apparent conflict between 400 years and 4 generations in God's promise to Abram. Read it carefully against the backdrop of ensuing passages and you'll find that there were indeed 400 years from Abram to Moses and there were also 4 generations from Moses till the Israelites were finally settled in the Promised Land. The length of a generation is measured by the span of time from a man's birth till the birth of his first son, in Biblical times about 40 years. Moses lived through 3 of these, being about 40 years old when he fled to Midian after killing an Egyptian soldier, 80 when he returned to confront Pharoah, and 120 when he died on Mt. Nebo just across the Jordan from the Promised Land. The generation of Israelites who crossed the Jordan and conquered the land were the 4th since the parents of Moses learned of his impending birth, those who left Egypt with him having all perished in the desert as a consequence of their disobedience (**Deut. 1:35**).

As for Moses killing an Egyptian for beating a Hebrew slave and then criticizing a fellow Hebrew for doing the same thing (**Ex. 2:11-14**), I believe Moses knew from his mother's vision that he was Israel's redeemer. This helps explain his behavior; acting in his own strength to begin their deliverance, and the slave's retort, "Who made you ruler and judge over us?" God had a better plan but now His chosen one was a murderer and fugitive from the law. His grace abounds even in sin, so Moses found refuge in the desert while those in Egypt either died or forgot him.

When he returned the Prince of Egypt was a nobody shepherd from Midian, acting in the strength of the Lord. And though Pharoah called himself a god, Moses was now more than a match for him. While each of the 10 plagues was aimed at one of the gods of Egypt, the last one was reserved for the man who called himself god.

As for the 10 nations whose land God had promised to Abraham's descendants, their sin was now complete. After 400 years of waiting in vain for them to repent and return to Him, the One who made them and loved them had run out of patience. Soon His armies would cross the Jordan and exact the punishment God always demands of those who refuse His grace and mercy (**Deut. 18:9-13**). Israel would fight the only war of aggression in their entire history, and receive the land He promised them as their everlasting reward.

Now you know the adult version.

The Passover ... Exodus 12

The descendants of Israel had been in Egypt nearly 400 years, and toward the end of that time were being greatly oppressed. A Pharaoh who didn't remember how Joseph had saved Egypt and made it the most powerful nation on Earth was now in charge (**Acts 7:18**). He was fearful of this foreign minority that seemed to be growing at an alarming rate. To help keep things under control, he brought in troops to force the Israelites into slavery making bricks for his huge construction projects. Then he ordered their midwives to kill all the male babies as they were born. But they tricked him, and now one of those baby boys who should have died had grown up to become a powerful leader, demanding, DEMANDING, that Pharaoh set them free.

Pharaoh thought himself a god, and was not about to knuckle under to a mere man, a Hebrew slave at that. It took 10 plagues, supernatural judgments from the God of the Hebrews, to change his mind. The first nine plagues brought destruction on Egypt from which they never recovered, with most of their crops and livestock destroyed, their drinking water turned to blood, and their bodies racked with pain from infestation and disease.

But it was the 10th one that really did them in. Earlier, the Lord had told Moses what his final plague would be. "Israel is my first born son, and if you don't let my people go I'll take your first born son." (**Ex. 4:22-23**). Now Moses angrily told Pharaoh what the fate of Egypt would be (**Ex. 11:1-10**).

The Passover

That day the Lord gave Moses special instructions for the Hebrews, and anyone else who wanted to be saved, to follow. On the 10th of the month they were to select a year old male lamb from among the flocks, one for each family. From the 10th till the 14th they were to inspect it carefully to be sure it was without defect or blemish. Then at twilight on the 14th they were to slaughter the lamb and roast it over an open fire. They were to paint its blood on the doorpost and lintel of their homes.

When the lamb was ready, each family was to eat the meat along with some bitter herbs (horse-radish) and some bread baked without yeast. Breaking no bones in the process and burning any leftovers, they were to eat standing up, packed and ready for a rapid departure. That same night the destroying angel would come through Egypt to take every first born from among the families of Egypt. As he did, the destroying angel would look at the door of each home and where he saw the lamb's blood, he would "pass over" that home sparing those inside. Where there was no blood, the first born would die. And so it was.

About midnight the first born of every home not marked by the blood of the lamb died. During the remainder of the night the Egyptians pleaded with the Hebrews to leave, gladly handing over all their personal wealth and possessions, which the Hebrews required of them as an inducement to go. And from that day to this, the Passover is celebrated annually in every Jewish home in commemoration of that event.

Christ In The Passover

Christians in growing numbers also celebrate the Passover today. We do so because of the unmistakable hints of the Messiah evident in the Passover Story. The Hebrews were saved by the blood of the lamb but only after applying it over their doors. Obviously, Jesus is the true Lamb of God (**John 1:29**). And as it was with them, it isn't the sacrifice of the Lamb of God that saves us, but the application of His blood to the doorposts of our hearts.

In addition as they painted each doorpost and lintel they were unknowingly making the sign of the cross, down and across, down and across. The lambs were roasted on a vertical spit with the lamb fastened upright by its forelegs to a cross bar on the spit, another clear model of the cross. And not just the Hebrews, but anyone in Egypt who applied the blood to their homes was saved.

On the morning of the 14th and for seven days

thereafter, they ate unleavened bread, instituting the seven-day Feast of Unleavened Bread (**Ex. 12:15-17**). For the next seven days the camp of Israel was rendered completely devoid of leaven. Leaven (we call it yeast) is a symbol of sin and seven the number of divine completeness. Ever since the true Lamb of God was sacrificed, all who apply His blood to their lives render themselves completely devoid of sin in God's eyes (**2 Cor. 5:17-21**).

The Biggest Miracle Of All

Taking the 600,000 men of military age (**Ex. 12:37**) and adding women, children and the elderly, somewhere between 1.5 and 2 million Hebrews left Egypt that morning. None was left behind. Think about that for a minute. 1.5 million people approximates the population of a fair sized city. What's the likelihood that in any city of that size on any given day all its inhabitants would be fit for a rigorous journey on foot? And don't forget, many of these people were overworked and undernourished slaves. Wouldn't sickness and injury be more likely among them than average folks? I believe the Lord supernaturally healed all their sick and injured that morning, probably the largest mass healing in human history.

And so the blood of the lamb did a lot more than just save them from the destroyer. The lame walked, the wounded were made whole, the sick were healed, the prisoners went free, the oppressed were released, and the poor became rich. Sounds just like what Jesus came to do for us.

Now you know the adult version.

Crossing the Red Sea

When Pharoah let the people go, God did not lead them on the road through the Philistine country though that was shorter. For God said if they face war they might change their minds and return to Egypt. So God led the people around by the desert road toward the Red Sea (**Exodus 13:17-18**).

Tracing the route the Israelites took in their Exodus from Egypt has often caused confusion among students of this miraculous event. We'll use the Bible to help clarify things.

The easiest way to determine the route is to locate the various destinations mentioned, first the Red Sea itself and then of course Mt. Sinai. For the Red Sea let's have a look at **1 Kings 9:26**. "King Solomon also built ships at Ezion Geber which is near Elath in Edom on the shore of the Red Sea."

As you look at a map of Egypt, The Red Sea vaguely resembles the head of a rabbit whose ears define the Sinai Peninsula, called the Desert of Sin in Biblical times. The left ear is the Gulf of Suez and the right one the Gulf of Aqaba. Elath is modern Eilat on the north east shore of the Gulf of Aqaba. on the border between Israel and Jordan. It's a beautiful resort famous for its bathing and diving due to the crystal clear waters and warm temperatures. You can still see some of the pillars erected by King Solomon in nearby Ezion Geber.

Since the shores of the Red Sea are often steep and the waters very deep the controversy over the location of the crossing stems partly from scholars' inability to find a convenient spot. This is compounded by an incorrect location for Mt. Sinai and has led to a search for alternate places including the marshes of the Nile Delta region. None of these fit when compared with Biblical passages.

Did God Really Say ... ?

Funny how our inability to understand God's methods will lead us to doubt His Word. We don't understand how He created the world in 6 days so we assume He didn't and look for alternate explanations to support our assumptions. We don't understand how He can know the end from the beginning so we assume He doesn't and spiritualize away the 40% of the Bible that's predictive prophecy. It seems like some scholars are forever telling us, "Here's what God really said", or "Here's what really happened." But "My thoughts are not your thoughts neither are your ways my ways" declares the Lord (**Isa. 55:8**). If God said something happened a certain way, it must be true and if we search long and hard enough we'll find confirmation. One of the great benefits of adhering to a literal interpretation of Scripture is discovering how well the Bible interprets and explains itself. When we seek Him with all our heart (**Prov 8:17**) and search the Scriptures diligently (**Acts 17:11**) we always find confirmation of His Word.

Mt. Sinai ... a Case in Point

When Constantine converted to Christianity back in the early 300's his mother Queen Helena did as well and, based on dreams she had, went through out the Middle East "locating" various Holy Places. Among them was Mt. Sinai, which she placed in the Desert of Sin resulting in the region being called the Sinai Peninsula. Several facts from the Bible argue against this. First, the area is not a suitable encampment for the number of people Moses led out of Egypt (over 1 million). It lacks both sufficient space and a source of water. Second, though they spent years at the foot of Mt. Sinai not a speck of evidence has ever been found to confirm their presence at Helena's location. Third the Sinai Peninsula is in Egypt on the wrong side of the Red Sea, and from history we know that it was regularly patrolled by Egyptian troops due to mining operations they had there. In spite of this, for hundreds of years Scholars have clung to her opinion. There's even a large monastery atop the mountain. Instead of concluding they had the wrong spot based on Biblical accounts, they've discounted the Word of God; and since they can't find supporting evidence where they're looking, some even doubt whether the event ever took place.

Meanwhile on the other side of the Red Sea in Saudi Arabia there's a mountain burned black on the top (**Ex. 19:18**) that Arabs have known about for centuries. It's called Jabal al Lawz or Jabal Mousa (Mountain of Moses). Nearby are the grave of Jethro, priest of Midian and father-in-law of Moses, (**Ex 18:1**) and the springs of Elim with their 70 palms (**Ex 15:27**). At the foot of this mountain boundary pillars can be found (**Ex 19:12**) along with an altar and an enormous split rock with a huge catch basin at its foot large enough to contain a small lake of fresh water (**Ex 17:5-7**). There's even an Egyptian petroglyph depicting a golden calf. Saudi Arabia was once called Midian and is on the eastern side of the Red Sea across the water from Egypt right where Mt. Sinai belongs. So now comes the question, how did they get across?

A Bridge Under Troubled Waters

At the tip of the Sinai Peninsula, in the Gulf of Aqaba, there's a remarkable clue. The water is very deep all around and the banks slope off sharply along most of its shoreline, but in the Straits of Tiran lies an abandoned freighter. Nearby there's a small beach area on both sides of the sea where it narrows considerably just at the entrance to the gulf. This caught the attention of American explorer Bob Cornuke, who was there looking for the real Mt. Sinai using Biblical accounts as his guide. Donning snorkel gear he headed into the crystal clear water for a closer look. As he stepped off the beach he expected to descend rapidly into deep water like he had every where else along the coast. But here he found himself walking out into water that only gradually became deeper. This explained the presence of the abandoned freighter. It had run aground. The water is several hundred feet deep all around, but beneath the Straits of Tiran there's an underwater land bridge connecting Egypt and Saudi Arabia, ancient Midian. The water covering this bridge, called Jackson Reef, never exceeds 40 feet in depth. When God brought the Israelites here Pharoah thought he had them cornered. But the Creator of the Universe swept the waters back revealing the land bridge He had made just for this purpose. As Pharoah's army pursued the Israelites, God let the waters roll back and drowned them all. A few days walk north on the eastern shore brought them to Mt. Sinai in modern Saudi Arabia. From there it's a straight shot north skirting the land of Edom to the eastern shores of the Jordan across from Jericho.

Now you know the adult version.

The Ten Commandments

And the Lord said to Moses, "Go to the people and consecrate them today and tomorrow. Have them wash their clothes and be ready by the third day because on that day the Lord will come down on Mt. Sinai in the sight of all the people." On the morning of the third day there was thunder and lightning with a thick cloud over the mountain and a very loud trumpet blast. Everyone in the camp trembled. Then Moses led the people out of the camp to meet with God and they stood at the foot of the mountain. Mt. Sinai was covered with smoke because the Lord descended on it in fire. The smoke billowed up from it like smoke from a furnace and the whole mountain trembled violently and the sound of the trumpet grew louder and louder. Then Moses spoke and the voice of God answered him. **(Exodus 19:10-11 and 16-19)**

In the following verses God gave the children of Israel His Ten Commandments (not suggestions), basic laws that were later expanded into a total of 613 in the Torah (5 Books of Moses). In a coming chapter I will share my view that the giving of the Commandments was part 2 of God's four part rebuttal to an accusation Satan had hurled at Him before the beginning of time (read "The Adversary"). I have also noted the incredible similarity between the details surrounding the giving of the law and the Rapture of the Church (read "Moses, Jesus and the Rapture" on our website at www.gracethrufaith.com).

When asked which were the greatest of all these laws, Jesus replied, "Love the Lord your God with all your heart and with all your soul and with all your mind (**Deut 6:5**). This is the first and greatest commandment and the second is like it: Love your neighbor as yourself (**Lev 19:18**). All the Law and Prophets hang on these two commandments" (**Matt 22:37-40**)." The phrase Law and Prophets referred to the entire Old Testament, but those two commandments particularly summarize the ten given at Mt. Sinai. The first four define how we should love the Lord our God (four is the number of Creation), and the last six how we demonstrate love for each other (six is the number of man).

God Is The Same, Yesterday, Today, And Forever (Hebr 13:8)

Although He required the Israelites to obey His commandments, the Bible has said all along that they were given to expose the motives of man's heart and show his need for a Savior. God's standard is simply too high for sinful man to achieve. The Old

Testament sacrifice of innocent animals pointed to this coming Savior whose Blood alone would purchase their pardon and was meant to confirm their need for Him. The Lord Jesus made this abundantly clear in His Sermon on the Mount when He explained that even thinking about violating the law is tantamount to doing so. He also made it clear that He hadn't come to abolish the law but rather to fulfill it (**Matt 5:17-18**). God's laws are still in force, we are still subject to them, and Jesus is the ransom for our souls as well as theirs.

Through out the Old Testament the true purpose of the law is explained. The prophet Micah asked, "With what shall I come before the Lord and bow down before the exalted God? Shall I come before Him with burnt offerings, with calves a year old? Will the Lord be pleased with 1000's of rams, with 10,000 rivers of oil? Shall I offer my first born for my transgression, the fruit of my body for the sin of my soul?" (**Micah 6:6-7**) The Lord had Micah give this answer. "He has showed you, O man, what is good. And what does the Lord require of you? To act justly, and to love mercy and walk humbly with your God (**Micah 6:8**)." Only by loving the Lord with all their heart and soul and mind and then loving their neighbors as themselves could they hope to accomplish this and no amount of external compliance with the law could suffice in its absence.

King David, after committing adultery with Bathsheba and causing the death of her husband, prayed, "Have mercy on me O God according to your unfailing love; according to your great compassion blot out my transgressions. Wash away all my iniquity and cleanse me from my sin. You do not delight in sacrifice or I would bring it; you do not take pleasure in burnt offerings. The sacrifices of God are a broken spirit. A broken spirit and a contrite heart O God You will not despise. (**Psalm 51: 1-2 and 16-17**).

David admitted that he had broken the law. But he knew that with sincerity and humility he could ask for and receive forgiveness, and that God would prefer this to an empty gesture of sacrifice. The prophet Nathan later explained to David that he could be forgiven in Heaven but that didn't necessarily relieve him of the earthly consequences of his behavior (**2 Sam 12:1-12**). (Those who run around saying, "I'm under grace not the law," would do well to remember this.)

Everything That Was Written The Past Was Written To Teach Us (Rom 15:4).

The children of Israel had promised to do "everything the Lord has said" (**Ex 19:8**). Yet before Moses could get down off the mountain with the 10 commandments they had broken most of them. Centuries later Paul admonished us, "Therefore no one will be declared righteous in His sight by observing the Law, rather through the law we become conscious of sin. (**Rom 3:20**). Just as a speed limit sign lets us compare our speed with the legal limit, the Commandments let us compare our behavior with God's requirements. When we're exceeding the speed limit the sign prompts us to slow down. When we're not meeting

God's requirements the Law prompts us to seek forgiveness.

Now you know the adult version.

And the Walls Came Tumblin' Down

On the 10th day of the first month the people went up from the Jordan and camped at Gilgal on the eastern border of Jericho. At that time the Lord said to Joshua, "Make flint knives and circumcise the Israelites again." On the evening of the 14th day of the month, while camped at Gilgal on the plains of Jericho the Israelites celebrated the Passover. The day after Passover, that very day, they ate some of the produce of the land; unleavened bread and some roasted grain. The manna stopped the day after they ate this food from the land. There was no longer any manna for the Israelites, but that year they ate of the produce of Canaan (**Josh 4:19, 5:2,10-12**).

Water Works

The crossing of the Jordan was at least as big a miracle as the crossing of the Red Sea. The Jordan

River was at flood stage that spring, but the Lord stopped the flow of the river so that the water piled up upon itself and the whole nation crossed over on dry ground (**Josh 3:13-17**). A column of people 400 abreast would have required all day to cross while the flood waters piled up higher and higher. When the kings of the various tribes inhabiting the land heard about this "their hearts melted and they no longer had the courage to face the Israelites" (**Josh 5:1**).

You have to admire the Lord's show of strength here. This rag tag army of desert nomads was closely watched as they arrived on the East Bank of the Jordan. No doubt the Amorite kings felt secure since the flooding and swollen river separated them from this strange group. But the Lord, Who ordained the laws of nature in the first place, simply overruled one of them and caused the river to stop flowing. Imagine the looks on the faces of those watching this grand spectacle. And when they had crossed, did the Lord send them into battle formation and prepare them to face the fiercest enemy in all the land? No, they camped in full view of the enemy, enjoyed some of the produce of the land, *and had all their fighting men circumcised.*

Four days later, having healed somewhat, they celebrated Passover for only the 3rd time in their history, and then they prepared for the coming battle. You have to suppose the inhabitants of Jericho just stood on the walls of their fortress and watched all this, too afraid to attack even while the Israelites were incapacitated. Makes me think of **Proverbs 16:7**: "When a man's ways are pleasing to the Lord,

He makes even his enemies live at peace with him."

A Man With A Plan

Now when Joshua was near Jericho, he looked up and saw a man standing in front of him with a drawn sword in his hand. Joshua went up to him and asked, "Are you for us or for our enemies?" "Neither", He replied, "But as the commander of the army of the Lord I have now come." Then Joshua fell face down to the ground in reverence and asked Him, "What message does the Lord have for His servant?" The commander of the Lord's army replied, "Take off your sandals for the place where you are standing is Holy." And Joshua did so (**Josh 5:13-15**).

Any doubt Joshua might have had about the identity of this Visitor was erased when he heard the same command previously given to Moses at the Burning Bush (**Ex 3:4-6**). Here was the Son of God in an Old Testament appearance, the Heavenly Joshua giving the earthly one his battle plan. And what a plan it was. (Joshua is Hebrew for Jesus).

Now Jericho was tightly shut up because of the Israelites. No one went out and no one came in. Then the Lord said to Joshua, "See I have delivered Jericho into your hands, along with its king and fighting men. March around the city once with all the fighting men. Do this for 6 days. Have 7 priests carry trumpets of rams' horns in front of the Ark. On the 7th day march around the city 7 times with the priests blowing the trumpets. When you hear them sound a long blast on the trumpets, have all the people give a loud shout; then the city wall will collapse and the people will go up, every man straight in" (**Josh 6:1-5**).

And so it was. At the sound of the trumpets on the 7th day and the 7th time around, the people shouted and the walls fell down. The Israelites marched in and destroyed every living thing in the city; the people, the animals, and all their possessions. The city was put to the torch and a curse pronounced over its ashes.

Spiritual Warfare

This battle was a Spiritual one. Joshua and the army of Israel were only along for the ride. The Lord wasn't on their side; they were on His. The first 6 times around the city was to show that with man alone the victory would be impossible (6 is the number of man, incomplete without God). The final seven showed that with God all things are possible. 6 (man) + 1 (God) = 7 (complete). The total of 13 circuits represents the apostasy of the inhabitants of Jericho that brought this judgment upon them. 13 is the number of apostasy or rebellion.

Remember the Lord's promise to Abraham. "Know for certain that your descendants will be strangers in a country not their own and they will be enslaved and mistreated 400 years. But I will punish the nation they serve as slaves, and afterward they will come out with great possessions. You however will go to your fathers in peace and be buried at a good old age. In the 4th generation your descendants will come back here for the sin of the Amorites has not yet reached its full measure." (**Gen 15:13-16**)

(By the way the 400 years and the 4th generation are 2 different things. For 400 years the
children of Israel lived in Egypt. But it was 4
generations from the promise of a deliverer to their
arrival in the land. In generation 1 Moses' birth and
destiny were foretold to his parents (**Hebr 11:23**).
As an adult Moses spent 40 years in Midian waiting for the people of his generation (2) to die so he
could go back to free the Israelites (**Ex 4:19**). The
people he freed, generation 3, had a crisis of faith
and died in the wilderness (**Num 14:31-35**). Their
children, generation 4, accompanied Joshua across
the Jordan to claim the land.)

Then there's the Lord's admonition to Israel in
the desert before they crossed the Jordan, "When you
enter the land the Lord your God is giving you, do
not learn to imitate the detestable ways of the nations
there. Let no one be found among you who sacrifices
his son or daughter in the fire, who practices divina-
tion or sorcery, interprets omens, engages in witch
craft, or casts spells, or who is a medium or spiritist,
or who consults the dead. Anyone who does these
things is detestable to the Lord and because of these
detestable practices the Lord your God will drive out
those nations before you (**Deut 18:9-12**).

In the only war of aggression Israel has ever
fought, they were agents of God's judgment against a
people who had known the Lord but abandoned Him
for pagan idols. Having given them over 400 years to
repent of their detestable practices and return to Him,
He finally ran out of patience and brought judgment

against them. Referring to the people living in the land, He commanded the Israelites, "Do not leave alive anything that breathes" (**Deut 20:16-18**). In describing the conditions there He had said, "Even the land was defiled, so I punished it for its sin and the land vomited out its inhabitants (**Leviticus 18:25**). Had the Israelites been faithful to this command, many of the problems they face today would have been avoided (**Judges 2:1-3**).

Now you know the adult version.

The Gospel in Joshua ...
The Story of Rahab)

The similarities between the Books of Joshua and Revelation are striking. In fact some call Joshua a model for Revelation, especially where it describes the battle of Beth Horon in chapter 10. The Israelites were confronted by a coalition of 5 Amorite kings led by someone who called himself Adoni-zedek, or Lord of Righteousness (a model of the anti-christ?). There were signs in the sun and moon as in **Rev. 6:12, 8:12**, and **16:8-11**, and large hailstones fell from the sky as in **Rev. 8:7** and **16:21**. The 5 Amorite kings hid in caves for fear of the Israelites just as in **Rev 6:15** the kings of the earth will hide in caves for fear of the wrath of the Lamb. At the end of Joshua, the land is dispossessed of its usurpers, at the end of Revelation the earth is dispossessed of its usurpers and as I indicated last time, the name Joshua is derived from the same Hebrew root as Yeshua, the Hebrew name for Jesus. But to me the most dramatic similarity is hidden in the story of Rahab. Hence the title of this chapter.

The Gospel in Joshua.

As the Israelites gathered along the east bank of the flooded and swollen Jordan, they were closely watched by the people of Jericho, only a short distance from the river's western shore. They had heard how the Lord had parted the Red Sea to allow the Israelites to escape the Egyptian army, and how He had helped them to utterly defeat the 2 Amorite kings east of the Jordan. In Rahab's own words, "When we heard of it our hearts melted and everyone's courage failed because of you for the Lord your God is God in heaven above and earth below." (**Josh 2:11**). Then the people of Jericho stood aghast as the God of Israel stopped the flow of the raging river, allowing His people to cross on dry ground.

When Joshua sent 2 spies into Jericho they found their way to Rahab's home and sought refuge there, which she granted in return for their guarantee of safety for her and her family. They agreed and told her that if she marked her home with a scarlet cord, she and anyone in the house with her would be spared in the coming battle (**Josh 2:12-21**). On the day of battle the city was captured and everyone within its walls died, except for Rahab and her family. She had gathered her family in her home and marked it with the scarlet cord as they had agreed. Before burning the city to the ground, Joshua had the 2 spies go to Rahab's home and bring her and all her family out to dwell among the Israelites. (**Josh 6:22-25**).

By the way, can you picture this? Her house was built into the city wall, which of course came tumbling down at the shout of the Israelite army. Of all the massive stone work protecting the city of Jericho, only that portion containing the home of Rahab was left standing. What a witness to the power of God, who "knows how to rescue Godly men from trials, and to hold the unrighteous for the Day of Judgment while continuing their punishment" (**2 Peter 2:9**). (See also **1 Thes. 1:10**)

By Grace We Are Saved, Through Faith

The name Rahab means proud, but among the people of Jericho, all of whom knew of the God of Israel, only Rahab humbled herself before the 2 spies and confessed Him as "God in Heaven above and Earth below." And speaking of the spies, what about them? Except for reporting that all the people of Jericho were scared to death did the spies bring Joshua any intelligence that helped develop the battle plan? No, the Lord had already determined the battle plan and they contributed nothing to it (**Josh 6:2-5**). So what was their true purpose in His plan? Seems like they were really 2 witnesses sent to hear Rahab's confession, save her from destruction, and give her a place among the Lord's people.

From that time on, Rahab dwelt with the Israelites. She married a man from the tribe of Judah named Salmon and had a son whom they named Boaz. Boaz took a gentile bride from Moab named Ruth and they had a son named Obed, who had a son named Jesse who had a son named David who became King of Israel (**Ruth 4:13-22**). And 26 generations later, two distant cousins who were both descendants of King David (and therefore of Rahab and Salmon) married and became the earthly parents of our Lord Jesus. And so when you read the genealogy of Jesus in Matthew, you'll find Rahab listed there (**Matt 1:5**).

It's Not What You Know, But Who You Know That Matters

Everyone in Jericho had heard about the God of Israel and all but Rahab and her family were destroyed on the day of battle. Rahab's faith saved her. When she believed in her heart that only One Who is God in Heaven above and Earth below could have done the things she had heard about, He went to great lengths to reveal Himself to her, sending 2 witnesses to testify of His power and love. Immediately after confessing Him as God, she was marked with a sign that guaranteed her security (**Ephe. 1:13-14**), called out from all the others in Jericho (**Rom. 8:29-30**), hidden on the day of battle (**Isa. 26:20-21 & Rev. 3:10**), and brought alive into the family of the Redeemer (**1 Thes. 4:16-17**). Just like you and me.

Now you know the adult version.

Samson and Delilah

A certain man of Zorah named Manoah from the clan of the Danites had a wife who was sterile and remained childless. The angel of the Lord appeared to her and said, "You are sterile and child-less, but you are going to conceive and have a son. Now see to it that you drink no wine or other fermented drink and that you do not eat anything unclean because you will conceive and have a son. No razor may be used on his head because the boy is to be a Nazirite, set apart to God from birth, and he will begin the deliverance of Israel from the Philistines" (**Judges 13:2-5**). The woman gave birth to a boy and named him Samson (*sunshine*) He grew and the Lord blessed him. And the spirit of the Lord began to stir in him while he was in Mahaneh Dan, between Zorah and Eshtaol (**Judges 13:24-25**).

The story of Samson is one of the most popular of the children's Bible stories because Samson was a real live super hero, the world's first. We all know how he killed a lion with his bare hands (**Judges 14:6**) slew 1000 Philistines with the jaw bone of an ass (**Judges 15:14-16**) and wound up in the clutches of Delilah (her name means *languishing*)(**Judges 16**). She betrayed him to the Philistines by convincing him to cut his hair and they put out his eyes and imprisoned him. Later at a great feast honoring their god Dagon for helping them capture Samson, they brought him out of prison to perform for them. He had his guard lead him to a place between the central pillars of the stadium and asking the Lord for strength pushed the pillars over, collapsing the whole building and killing himself and all the Philistine leaders (**Judges 16:23-30**). No Saturday morning cartoon ever had more drama, action, and victory over seemingly overwhelming odds.

Hair Today, Gone Tomorrow

But the story becomes even more fascinating when we search the Scriptures for clues to its deeper meaning. In **Numbers 6:1-8** the Lord gave Moses directions on the proper way to execute a special vow of separation called the Nazirite vow. As the angel had instructed Samson's parents, people taking the Nazirite vow could not cut their hair, drink any wine, or partake of any food or drink derived from grapes. Normally the vow was voluntary and kept for a period of time to demonstrate a commitment to God, after which the person returned to a normal life. But 3 times in Scripture the Lord designated a yet to be born child as a life long Nazirite. All 3 were born to previously barren women: Samson, Samuel (**1ˢᵗ Samuel:1**) who anointed David as Israel's king, and John the Baptist (**Luke 1**), who proclaimed the coming Messiah. Our Lord Jesus, by the way, was a Nazarine (from Nazareth) but not a Nazirite.

So have you figured out why Samson's supernatural strength failed when Delilah betrayed him to the Philistines? That's right, by letting her cut his hair he violated the Nazirite vow. His commitment to the Lord was broken and his strength gone because "the symbol of his separation to God is on his head" (**Numbers 6:7**). While *languishing* in prison, he recommitted himself and grew his hair back, permitting the Lord to restore his supernatural power for one last feat of strength, fulfilling his life's purpose to begin Israel's deliverance from the Philistines (**Judges 13:5**).

Where is Palestine?

As an aside, the Philistines pronounced their name with a hard P, not with the soft PH or F sound we're used to, making it sound more like Palestine. When the Romans conquered Israel they re-named the land Palestine (Land of the Philistines) on their maps as an insult to the Jews. This insult has continued through the centuries and that's why some call Israel Palestine to this day. The Romans were just one of a long line of Gentile nations refusing to acknowledge Israel's right to the land, but some Palestinians use this connection with the Philistines as a basis for a claim to the land pre-dating the arrival of Joshua and the Israelites.

Is That You Lord?

But back to our story. Earlier, Manoah had inquired of the Angel of the Lord, "What is your name so that we may honor you when your word comes true?" He replied, "Why do you ask my name? It is beyond understanding." (**Judges 13:17-18**) The Hebrew word *pele* translated beyond understanding in the NIV is rendered Wonderful in the King James. It's the same word used in **Isaiah 9:6**. For unto us a child is born, and unto us a son is given and the government will be upon His shoulders. And He will be called Wonderful (*pele*), Counselor, Mighty God, Everlasting Father, Prince of Peace. I think Isaiah used these 5 titles to hint that the Messiah would personify the Trinity, being all God and all man. Mighty God and Everlasting Father are self-evident and Counselor is the name given the Holy Spirit in **John 14:25**. Prince of Peace always refers to the Lord Jesus, and I believe Wonderful refers Him as well. 5, the number of grace, indicates that the Messiah came to demonstrate God's Grace. If I'm right, the angel appearing to Manoah was the Lord Jesus in one of His many Old Testament appearances.

But to me the most remarkable lesson is the way in which Samson's life parallels the history of Israel. Both were set apart from birth, foretold by an angel, called to begin the deliverance of God's people, supernaturally empowered against overwhelming odds, sought after strange women (false gods), blinded for disobedience, called upon the Lord, and brought judgment upon His enemies.

Now you know the adult version.

David and Goliath

Now the Philistines gathered their forces for war and assembled in Socoh in Judah. They pitched camp at Ephes Dammim, between Socoh and Azekah. Saul and the Israelites assembled and camped in the valley of Elah and drew up their battle lines to meet the Philistines. The Philistines occupied one hill and the Israelites another, with the valley between them.

A champion named Goliath who was from Gath came out of the Philistine camp. He was over nine feet tall. He had a bronze helmet on his head and wore a coat of scale armor of bronze weighing 5000 shekels (125 lbs.), on his legs he wore bronze greaves (shin guards) and a bronze javelin was slung on his back. His spear shaft was like a weaver's rod and its iron point weighed 600 shekels (15 lbs.) His shield bearer went ahead of him.

Goliath stood and shouted to the ranks of Israel, "Why do you come out and line up for battle? Am I not a Philistine and are you not servants of Saul? Choose a man and have him come down to me. If he is able to fight and kill me then we will be your subjects. But if I overcome him and kill him then you will become our subjects and serve us."

Then the Philistine said, "This day I defy the ranks of Israel. Give me a man and let us fight each other."

On hearing the Philistine's words, Saul and all the Israelites were dismayed and terrified. For 40 days the Philistine came forward every morning and every evening and took his stand (**1 Sam 17:1-11, 16**).

And a Little Child Shall Lead Them

David was the youngest of the 8 sons of Jesse. The 3 oldest had followed Saul to war, and as was the custom of the time David being too young to enlist carried food and other supplies to his brothers in support of the war effort.

One morning he arrived at the Israelite camp in time to hear Goliath's daily challenge to the men of Israel. "Who is this uncircumcised Philistine that he should defy the armies of the Living God," he demanded (**1 Sam 17:26**). Even though the prophet Samuel had already visited Jesse's home and anointed David as Israel's next King, (**1 Sam 16:13**) to his brothers he was still a little kid come to embarrass them, and they tried to send him home.

But King Saul heard of David's questions and sent for him. David said to Saul, "Let no one lose heart on account of this Philistine, your servant will go out and fight him" (**1 Sam 17:32**). When Saul reminded David that he was just a boy, David recalled the times while tending sheep when the flock had been attacked by both bear and lion, and David had defeated them. "The Lord Who delivered me from the paw of the lion and the paw of the bear will deliver me from the hand of this Philistine," he declared. Saul said to David, "Go, and the Lord be with you"(**I Sam 17:37**).

We all know how David, armed with only a sling-shot, fired a stone into Goliath's forehead and killed him. And how the Israelites chased the Philistine army all the way back to the gates of their cities, completing Israel's deliverance from Philistine bondage, a task Samson had begun earlier (**Judges 13:5**). But as exciting as this story is on the surface, there is even more hidden beneath.

I Spoke To The Prophets, Gave Them Many Visions And Told Parables Through Them ... Hosea 12:10

Several times in Scripture, the Lord informs us of the value of these stories from Israel's history (**Rom 15:4 & 1 Cor 10:11**). We're to learn the lessons they contain, not just repeat them as histori-cal accounts, because they were orchestrated in such a way as to reveal truths about God, and none more so than the story of David and Goliath.

If you see the story as a parable on spiritual warfare, you'll gain some remarkable insight. The word parable means to "lay along side" so we're not discarding the historical validity of the account, just gaining another level of understanding.

The main characters in Biblical parables always represent someone or something else, so try seeing Goliath and the Philistines as Satan and his demonic host, Saul and the Israelites as man in the flesh, and David as man in the Spirit.

For 40 days Saul and his army were intimidated and paralyzed by the defiant words of Goliath, just as in the flesh man is intimidated and paralyzed by the power of Satan. 40 is the Biblical number of testing and shows that man in the flesh will always fail his test with the enemy. And as David discovered, not even the king's own armor, the best man could fashion, was suitable protection but instead further encumbered and immobilized him (**1 Sam 17:38-39**).

Our struggle is not against flesh and blood, but against the rulers, against the authorities, against the powers of this dark world, and against the spiritual forces of evil in the heavenly realms (**Ephe 6:12**). For though we live in the world, we do not wage war as the world does. The weapons we fight with are not the weapons of the world. On the contrary they have divine power to demolish strongholds (**2 Cor 10:3-4**).

Wearing Saul's armor, David was an awkward and ineffective boy, but armed in the strength of the Lord he was more that a match for the giant Goliath (**1 Sam 17:45-47**). "Not by might, nor by power, but by My Spirit," says the Lord Almighty (**Zech 4:6**).

Logic vs. Emotion

It's good to remember that there was logic to David's position, and not just emotion. Sure he was indignant at Goliath's defiance of the Lord's Army and angry that no Israelite had accepted the challenge, but the Lord had already used him to defeat a lion and a bear, either of which could have been a match for Goliath. And he had been anointed as Israel's next king, an unconditional promise God could not fulfill if David was defeated and killed. So David had his own past experience and the promise of One who cannot lie to bolster his faith. Knowing these things, he didn't believe the possibility of defeat existed (**1 Sam 17:32-37**).

Parables have often been described as heavenly stories put into an earthly perspective. To gain their wisdom, just put things back into the spiritual realm. Doing so we find that we have the same logical support for our faith that David had for his. The Lord has already defeated His enemy and ours (**Col. 2:15 & 2 Tim 1:10**) and we've been promised not only kingship (**Ephe 2:6-7**) but also sonship (**Gal 4:4-5**) by the one who cannot lie. These are unconditional promises that God cannot fulfill if we can be overcome and defeated by our enemy. Knowing these things, we can't logically believe the possibility of defeat exists. Fear and faith cannot dwell in the same mind at the same time. Submit yourselves then, to God. Resist the devil and he will flee from you (**James 4:7**) just as the Philistines fled from the Israelites.

By the way when David went out to face Goliath he stooped down and picked up 5 smooth stones (**1 Sam 17:40**). Ever wonder why? It turns out Goliath had 4 brothers. (**2 Sam 21:18-22 KJV**)

Now you know the adult version.

Elijah on Mt. Carmel

So (King) Ahab sent word throughout all Israel
and assembled the prophets on Mount Carmel.
Elijah went before the people and said, "How long
will you waver between two opinions? If the Lord is
God follow Him, but if Baal is God follow him"
(**1 Kings 18:21**)

A Little Background Please

As King David's life was drawing to a close, the
Lord chose his son Solomon to succeed him. It was
the time of Israel's closest approximation to the
Messianic Kingdom promised by God. There was
peace in the land and Israel's influence in the world
was with out equal. Kings from every land came and
paid homage to Solomon, whose wisdom was
legendary. Solomon reigned in peace and prosperity
for 40 years but toward the end of his reign began to
pay the price for his one act of disobedience. The
Lord had forbidden the Israelites from marrying

foreign women, knowing that they would bring pagan gods into Israel and lead their husbands into false religion (**1 Kings 11:2**).

In violation of the Lord's prohibition Solomon had taken 700 wives and 300 concubines, many of them foreign, and had permitted them to worship their own gods, even building idols of some on a hill east of Jerusalem. This angered the Lord and caused a civil war in Israel that resulted in the Kingdom being divided. Following the death of Solomon, the Northern Kingdom, called Israel and consisting of the land given to 10 of the 12 tribes, descended rapidly into idol worship while the smaller Southern Kingdom, called Judah and consisting of the land given to the remaining 2 tribes, remained faithful to God.

During this time all those in the Northern Kingdom who remained faithful to God migrated south with the Levites (**2 Chron 11:16**) so all the 12 tribes were represented in the Southern Kingdom. The notion of 10 tribes being lost following the subsequent defeat of the Northern Kingdom by Assyria is not Scriptural, and any doctrine based on the so-called lost 10 tribes is therefore suspect. But that's a topic for another day.

How Long Will You Waver Between Two Opinions?

For the next 80 years the people of the Northern Kingdom vacillated between allegiance to God and allegiance to various Canaanite deities, sometimes worshipping all of them at the same time. During

Elijah's time there had been a drought in Israel for 3 years, a sign of God's displeasure with this ongoing flirtation with paganism. Ahab was King of Israel and had married a daughter of the King of neighboring Phoenicia (Lebanon), a powerful and influential woman named Jezebel. She personally supported 450 prophets of Baal and 400 prophets of Asherah. It was these prophets that Ahab summoned to Mt. Carmel in response to Elijah's "invitation". In the presence of all the people Elijah (his name means God is Lord) had challenged the prophets of Baal to a contest designed to reveal the one true God.

Elijah said to them, "I am the only one of the Lord's prophets left, but Baal has 450 prophets. Get 2 bulls for us. Let them choose one for themselves and let them cut it into pieces and put it on the wood but not set fire to it. I will prepare the other bull and put it on the wood but not set fire to it. Then you call on the name of your god and I will call on the name of the Lord. The god who answers by fire – He is God." Then all the people said, "What you say is good." (**1 Kings 18:22-24**)

All that morning the prophets of Baal called upon their god. They danced around their altar, and cut themselves with knives, part of their religious practice. At noon Elijah began to taunt them. "Shout louder," he said, "Surely he is a god. Perhaps he is relieving himself or busy or traveling. Maybe he is sleeping and must be awakened" (**1 Kings 18:27**). This went on all through the day with no response from Baal. Then at the time of the evening sacrifice Elijah took 12 stones, one for each of the 12 tribes of

Israel, and built an altar for the Lord. He dug a trench around it and placed wood upon it. He cut the other bull into pieces and arranged them on the wood. Then he had the people bring 4 large jars filled with water that he poured on the offering and the wood. "Do it again," he said and they did. "Do it a 3rd time," he ordered and they did. The water ran down around the altar and filled the trench. And then he prayed. "O Lord, God of Abraham, Isaac and Israel, let it be known today that You are God in Israel, and that I am your servant and have done all these things at your command. Answer me O Lord, answer me, so these people will know that You O Lord are God and that You are turning their hearts back again" (**1 Kings 18:36-37**). Talk about a grand-stand play. Can't you just feel the tension mounting each time the altar was doused?

Then the fire of the Lord fell and burned up the sacrifice, the wood, the stones and the soil and even licked up the water in the trench. When the people saw this they fell prostrate and cried, "The Lord – He is God. The Lord – He is God"(**1 Kings 18:39**. Elijah had them seize the pagan prophets and execute them according to Mosaic law (**Deut 13:1-5**) and shortly thereafter rain fell on the land of Israel for the first time in 3 years, a sign of God's pleasure. Jezebel swore out a death curse on Elijah but God took him alive into heaven. The people later abandoned God again, judgment came in the form of the Assyrian armies, and the Northern Kingdom ceased to exist.

Your Mission, Should You Choose To Accept It ...

At the close of the Old Testament, the Lord promised that Elijah would return to earth to herald the coming Messiah. He would once again turn the hearts of the fathers to their children and the hearts of the children to their fathers, or else God would strike the land with a curse (**Mal 4:5-6**). Jesus said that John the Baptist was the promised Elijah (**Matt 17:11-13**), and although the hearts of many were turned to God King Herod put him to death. 38 years later the land was struck with a curse, judgment came in the form of the Roman armies and the Nation Israel ceased to exist.

At the end of the age, Elijah will once again bring drought upon the earth at the Lord's command, and for the 3rd time will implore the people to repent of their sins, and again the hearts of many will be turned to God. The antichrist will think he's put him to death, but again God will take him live into heaven (**Rev. 11:11-12**). Judgment will come in the form of the Lord's armies and the world as we know it will cease to exist.

This Is Your Last Chance

Elijah used 4 jars of water to douse the altar 3 times. 4 is the number of the earth (by the end of the 4th day its creation was complete) and the water can represent the pouring out of the Holy Spirit (see **John 7:37-39**). If so then the three dousings of the altar hint at Elijah's three missions to earth offering God's Holy Spirit and imploring the people to turn their hearts back to Him. After limited success each one ends in failure and is followed by a judgment. Each time the Lord in His mercy provides His people another chance.

The Millennium is man's last chance; there is no 4th mission for Elijah. But at the end of the Millennium in spite of utopian conditions with Satan bound and 1000 years of personal rule by the Lord Jesus Himself, there's still enough residual evil in the heart of unregenerate man for Satan to mount a rebellion as soon as he's freed (**Rev 20:7-10**). This illustrates man's total inability to remain faithful to God. In spite of 7000 years of history filled with the undeniable revelations of God's existence and His endless patience in dealing with us, only the shed blood of Jesus is able to make us fit to dwell in His presence.

Now you know the adult version.

The Adversary Part 1 ...
The Shining One

◄─═◯═►

Let's pause in our series on Children's Stories to get a better look at the great adversary who stands behind every effort to thwart God's will in these events. Since he is a created being (**Eze. 28:13**) whose creation is not mentioned in the Genesis account we'll assume that he was created along with the other angelic beings, in the gap between **Gen. 1:1** and **1:2** (see chapter 1, In The Beginning). All we know by way of introduction is that he turns up in the Garden in the form of a "serpent" (the Hebrew means "enchanter") to beguile our first parents. But from **Isaiah 14:12-20** and **Ezekiel 28:11-19** we can piece together a profile of this great adversary, his origin, fall and destiny.

How You Have Fallen From Heaven, O Lucifer

His name comes from **Isaiah 14:12** (KJV). Lucifer is actually the Latin translation of a Hebrew phrase that means to shine in the sense of making a show or celebration or (foolish) boast and recalls the title "shining one." **Ezekiel 28:12-14** indicates he was created as "the model of perfection, full of wisdom and beauty" and anointed as the guardian cherub on the holy mount of God. In the Septuigent translation of the Hebrew scriptures all the stones contained on the breast plate of Israel's High Priest are listed in **Eze 28:13** perhaps hinting at his responsibilities. Combining the Ezekiel and Isaiah passages we can infer that he was head of the congregation of Angelic beings, charged with leading them in the worship of the Almighty and guardian of His Throne.

The "foolish boast" part of his name came to bear when wickedness was found in him (**Eze 28:15**). Excessively proud of his beauty and wisdom, he rebelled against God and uttered his infamous "five I will's" culminating in a declaration that he would make himself "like The Most High"(**Isa 14:13-14**). This was the first of countless repetitions caused by the sin nature of man that prompts him to emulate Lucifer, trying to become like God by exalting, glorifying and even deifying himself. The next time it happened was in the Garden when Adam & Eve were deceived into thinking they could "become like God"(**Gen. 3:5**).

Satan's rebellion brought judgment upon him and the seat of his throne, Planet Earth, leaving Earth an uninhabitable ruin for who knows how long. As I've said, many believe this all took place in the apparent gap between the first 2 verses of Genesis. If so it helps reconcile the conflict between a geologically proven old earth (10 billion years) and the Biblically described young civilization (6000 years). I should also note that recent measurements of the speed of light indicate that it may have been gradually slowing down over time. If that's proven true then all our speculation about the age of Earth's ancient past goes out the window. But that's another story.

Satan Is Alive And Well On Planet Earth

Hal Lindsey, is his book so titled speculates that at his judgment Satan hurled 2 accusations at God: "You're not just and You have no love." In response to these accusations God did the following.

1. He created man, a being vastly inferior to the angels but sharing with them the properties of intellect, agency (power of choice) and eternal life, and gave him dominion over Planet Earth.

2. He gave man a set of rules to live by, and ordained that obedience to them was a requirement for life. Any violations (sins), even those committed only in the mind, would be punishable by death. There were no loopholes, and no one would escape judgment. Perfect justice.

3. He sent His Son to live a life in total compliance with these rules, the only man ever to do so, granting Him the right to govern the universe and receive all its worth as His inheritance.

4. He gave His Son's life to purchase a pardon for all whose sins would require judgment, decreeing that by accepting His death as payment for their sins they would also receive eternal life and share in this inheritance as His adopted children. Perfect Love.

What Do You Say To That?

Satan's response to God's first action was to immediately steal control of Planet Earth and cause the contamination of the human gene pool with a sin nature making it impossible for man to obey God's rules, condemning us all to death. And then he used all his powers of deception to try and prevent us from ever learning about the pardon God had purchased for us. Or failing in that, to trick us into thinking we don't qualify by infiltrating the church (**2 Cor. 11:13-15**) to promote his false doctrine (**Gal 1:8, Col. 2:8, 1 Tim 4:1**). In that way he thinks he can cause so many to be condemned that God out of His love for us will have to bend His rules and overlook our sins. If He bends for man, He'll have to bend for Satan.

Satan is the god of this age (**2 Cor. 4:4**), and the prince of this world (**John 12:31, 14:30, 16:11**), having the whole world under his control (**1 John 5:19**). But the deceiver has deceived himself. Too proud to apologize to God, he thinks to defeat Him (foolish boast), even though his own defeat was determined at the cross (**Col. 2:13-15**). While the church currently restrains his authority over earth (**2 Thes, 2:5**), during the Great Tribulation he'll be free to do his worst. But it won't be enough and having been expelled from Heaven (**Rev 12:7**), he'll be bound in the Abyss for 1000 years (**Rev 20:1-3**) and finally cast into the eternal fire (**Rev 20:10**).

Now you know the adult version.

The Adversary Part 2 ...
I Will Make Myself Like
the Most High

How you have fallen from heaven, O Lucifer son of the dawn. You have been cast down to the earth, you who once laid low the nations. You said in your heart, "I will ascend to heaven. I will raise my throne above the stars of God. I will sit enthroned on the mount of the assembly, on the uttermost heights of the sacred mountain. I will ascend above the tops of the mountains. I will make myself like the Most High" (**Isaiah 14:12-14**).

What's Going On Here?

Was the one we call Satan trying to replace God or become a god himself? The key lies in the term "Most High." It's used for the first time in **Genesis 14:18-19,** where God is described as the Most High God, **possessor of heaven and earth** (KJV). Some of the modern translations substitute creator or maker for possessor, but the Hebrew favors the KJV. Normally *bara*, which means "to create" is used in referring to the Creator but in **Genesis 14:19** it's *qanah*. *Qanah* appears 82 times in Scripture and although it can mean create, it's not translated that way anywhere else in Scripture. It literally means to get or acquire and implies ownership.

Everything in the Universe belonged to the One who had created it and some speculate that He had permitted Satan to place his throne here on Earth. After all, Satan was an important dignitary among the principalities and powers in the heavenly realms (**Ezek. 28:14** and **Jude 8-10**). But although he wasn't the creator of heaven and earth he didn't want to be a mere tenant. He wanted to own the place outright and become a parallel focus of worship (becoming "like the Most High) so he rebelled against God causing the judgment we discussed last time.

Possessor Of Heaven And Earth?

This view makes the subsequent actions by both God and Satan more easily understood. Ever wonder why in all the 6 days of creation the only work God did not pronounce as good was on the second day, the creation of the heavens (**Gen 1:6-7**)? Remember there are 3 locations in the Bible called "heaven": the Earth's atmosphere, the vast reaches of space beyond, and the throne of God. The Hebrew word used in **Gen.1:1** and **6,7**. (KJV) is unusual in that it's a dual form, like our word both. It can only include 2 of whatever is being referenced, in this case "heavens".

So it describes our atmosphere and space beyond, omitting God's Throne.

That same Hebrew word for heaven is used in **Genesis 14:19.** And in **Ephesians 2:2** Paul refers to Satan as the "ruler of the kingdom of the air". The Greek word there means atmosphere. Could it be that upon the creation of the heavens Satan and his fellow rebels immediately invaded them preventing God from taking pleasure in that which He had just made? If so, Satan became the possessor of "heaven" at that time (squatter's rights?). This also explains why when Paul refers to being "caught up to paradise" (**2 Cor. 12:2-4**) he takes pains to call it the 3rd heaven, God's Throne.

Then, when God created Adam and gave him dominion over the earth, Satan's response was to steal it from him, since he had failed to get it from God, and become the possessor of Earth (**1 John 5:19**). In the wilderness temptation one of the things Satan offered our Lord was the authority and splendor of all the kingdoms of earth (**Matt 4:8-9**). You can't give what you don't own, but the Lord did not dispute Satan's claim of ownership, however flawed.

Your Mission, If You Choose To Accept It ...

The Lord's mission to earth was clearly foretold in the Old Testament. Satan realized that regaining the ownership of planet earth was a primary objective. That's why he was willing to negotiate it away in the wilderness temptation. After all he would still have the heavens and could still be worshipped, even by the Son of God. But then at the cross something happened that he hadn't foreseen (**Col. 2:13-15**). All Adam's children could now become God's, the sin problem overcome, and those who refused would do so by choice relieving God of any responsibility for them.

The Secret Rapture

And check this out. Very soon, at a date and hour still undisclosed, those who have chosen to become God's children will meet the Lord in the air (1st heaven) (**1 Thes 4:16-17**). Does the Lord intend the Rapture of the Church as a sneak attack to begin repossessing the heavens? Then at the beginning of the Great Tribulation Satan will be expelled from the 2nd heaven (**Rev 12:12**). And finally at the 2nd coming the Lord will set up his kingdom here having defeated Satan's armies. Now who's possessor of heaven and earth?

Surely this is why our Creator, the master of strategy, kept the rapture of the church secret until after the cross, completing the conversion of what Satan fore saw as a huge victory into his utter defeat. It's also why Paul was able to declare that none of the "rulers of this age" understood this for if they had they would not have crucified the Lord of Glory (**1 Cor 2:8**). Jesus spoke not a word of the Rapture to his disciples, but had Paul introduce it after it was too late for the enemy to react. It was a secret component of the Lord's strategy to totally reverse Satan's bid to become possessor of heaven and earth. **Now you know the adult version.**

Three Boys In The Fiery Furnace

After Assyria conquered the Northern Kingdom in 722BC all that was left of Israel was a small portion around Jerusalem called Judah. In spite of the judgment experienced by their cousins in the north, Judah also fell into a state of idolatry and so the Lord permitted Babylon to conquer them as well (**Jer. 25:8-9**). In his first siege of Jerusalem in 605BC the King of Babylon took hostages from the Royal family to his capital in an effort to assure the compliance of those he left in place as vassals to govern Judah according to his wishes. (This plan was ultimately unsuccessful and so in 586BC after 2 more sieges, he completely destroyed Jerusalem including the Temple Solomon had built and carried off all its inhabitants into slavery.)

Among the royal hostages were Daniel, a future prophet of Israel whom the King renamed Belteshazzar, and three friends, Hananiah, Mishael, and Azariah renamed Shadrach, Meshach and Abednego. These four were given training and education in the ways of Babylon and otherwise prepared to serve the King in his court (**Daniel 1:1-7**). They proved to be excellent students and within a few years, following Daniel's interpretation of a dream that had troubled the King, were appointed to positions of administrative authority over the Province of Babylon (**Daniel 2**).

You Shall Have No Other Gods Before Me

Sometime later the King decided to have a gigantic golden statue of himself placed in a prominent place on the plains of Dura outside the city. It was sixty cubits (90 ft.) tall 6 cubits wide and according to tradition stood on a pedestal six steps high and here you have the first clue of what's really going on in this children's story (666). The King required all his subjects to bow down and worship the statue and decreed that anyone refusing to do so would be thrown into a fiery furnace and burned alive (**Daniel 3:1-7**). It should be noted that the pagan rites of worship in Babylon included public acts of a sexual nature, a kind of "group grope".

Shadrach, Meshach, and Abednego had maintained their covenant relationship with the God of Israel and refused to bow down and worship anyone other than Him, especially since it included behavior that was forbidden under God's law. This act of disobedience was reported to the King and though fond of them he was furious. When they rejected his offer of a 2nd chance to comply with his command, saying that their God was able to rescue them but even if He didn't they still wouldn't worship anyone else, he had them bound and thrown into the furnace (**Daniel 3:16-23**) as he had threatened to do.

Apparently this furnace was constructed in a public place so that the punishment could be witnessed by all, because the King saw his three disobedient subjects in the fire. But he was shocked to see a 4th figure in there as well; one who looked like "the Son of God", and all four were walking around in the fire unbound (**Daniel 3:25**). The King called Shadrach, Meshach, and Abednego to come out of the furnace and to his utter amazement discovered that they were totally unharmed, not even the smell of smoke on their clothing, and the only things burned up were the ropes that had bound them. The King gave praise to the God of Israel and decreed that from that time on anyone who said anything against Him would be executed "for no other god can save in this way" (**Daniel 3:28-29**).

Types And Shadows

In addition to recounting an actual event from Israel's history and being a favorite of children for ages, this story prophesies of a time yet future to us. One day soon another world ruler will make an image of himself and require that every one in the world bow down and worship before it on pain of death (**Rev 13:13-18**). The King of Babylon therefore becomes a model for the antichrist, and the fiery furnace represents the Great Tribulation. Shadrach, Meshach, and Abednego fore shadow the remnant of

Israel preserved through the judgment (**Rev 12:13-14**) and freed from the bondage of their religion for a closer walk with their Messiah (**Zech. 12:10-11**)

Any Questions?

The often-unasked question regarding this story is "Where was Daniel?" Daniel and the King of Babylon had developed a special relationship starting from the time he had interpreted the King's dream. It was at Daniel's suggestion that Shadrach, Meshach, and Abednego were given positions of responsibility (**Daniel 2:49**). He was their benefactor and like them had remained faithful to his covenant with God. Yet he appears nowhere in this story. Daniel is one of only 2 Biblical characters about whom nothing critical is ever said (the other is Joseph) so it's unlikely that he bowed down and worshipped the statue. And since he had really embarrassed the other "wise men" in the King's court by being the only one who could interpret the King's dream, it's also hard to believe that they would let him get away with disobeying the King's command.

The only plausible explanation is that Daniel had gone away during this time, and perhaps it was his absence that gave the others the courage to report Shadrach, Meshach, and Abednego for their non-compliance. If so then Daniel becomes a remarkable type of the church whose disappearance before the tribulation begins removes us from the time and place of judgment (**Rev. 3:10**) releases the restraint against evil in the world (**2 Thes. 2:7**) and begins the time of Israel's greatest persecution (**Matt 24:21**).

You can't base a pre-tribulation rapture doctrine on this, but if you're already so inclined, the story of the three boys in the fiery furnace takes on added meaning. It becomes another one of those beautiful models the Lord has built to instruct and encourage us with events from Israel's history. For everything that was written in the past was written to teach us, so that through endurance and the encouragement of the Scriptures we might have hope (**Rom. 15:4**).

Now you know the adult version.

The Handwriting
On The Wall

Daniel was an old man in his eighties and retired from public service when he received the urgent message to report immediately to the Great Banquet Hall in Babylon, the city where he and his fellow Jews had been captive for nearly seventy years.

The Babylonian King Nebuchadnezzar had died some years ago, his son the current King was away in a remote part of the Kingdom, and so his grandson, Belshazzar was in charge. Daniel had become a close friend and advisor to Nebuchadnezzar, but didn't much care for this upstart grandson. The feeling was mutual.

Even though a massive army of Medes and Persians were camped outside the city wall, inside there was a party going on. In spite of the huge enemy force, or maybe to taunt them, Belshazzar had thrown this party for a thousand of his closest friends and their dates. The intent was to project a feeling of security inside the city while demoralizing the enemy troops outside.

Even without this attempt at psychological warfare, Babylon was a formidable challenge to any army. The city was 14 miles on a side, with walls 350 feet high and 87 feet thick. At strategic points along the walls hundreds of lookout towers rose an additional 100 feet into the desert air. The wide thoroughfare that ran along the top of the city wall was the scene of periodic chariot races, with sometimes as many as four chariots abreast racing at full speed for the prize.

The mighty Euphrates River ran through the city bringing all the fresh water they could use, and fields and pastureland inside the walls assured a steady supply of food. The Babylonians could survive in their fortress city indefinitely.

On top of that, huge bronze grated gates were lowered down into the river where it flowed under the city walls to deprive any would be enemy of access from the water. So the people had good reason to feel safe, hence the celebration. They thought the city was impregnable

As the party progressed and the wine flowed ever more freely, someone called for a toast, and soon everyone was thanking and praising the Babylonian gods they credited with protecting them. And as a further affront to the God of the Hebrews, Belshazzar called for the cups and goblets his grandfather had looted from the Temple in Jerusalem, and placed in the Babylonian museum, to be brought for use in toasting their pagan gods. It was a festive mood all right.

Suddenly the fingers of a human hand appeared and wrote on the plaster wall behind the King's head, near the lamp stand in the royal palace. The king watched the hand as it wrote. His face turned pale and he was so frightened that his knees knocked together and his legs gave way. **(Daniel 5:5-6)**

Well, that changed the mood all right. In the blink of an eye the place was as quiet as a church on Monday morning. Belshazzar called for his magicians to read the writing but no one could, even though he promised that anyone who did would become the third highest in the Kingdom, next to his father and himself. Belshazzar was really scared now. This hand appearing out of nowhere had been bad enough, but having written something no one could understand made it even worse. Who did this and what did they want?

Then Belshazzar's grandmother, widow of Nebuchadnezzar, hearing all the fuss came into the hall and suggested they go find the old Hebrew Prophet Daniel. She remembered how he had interpreted her husband's dreams years ago. Maybe he could solve this puzzle, too.

So Daniel was located and brought into the hall. When he saw the writing, he understood it immediately and so wasted no kindness or diplomacy on this boy who would be king. When offered the third spot in the hierarchy, he said "You may keep your gifts and give your rewards to someone else, nevertheless I will read the writing and tell you what it means." **(Daniel 5:17)**

Then he reminded the Belshazzar how incredibly powerful his grandfather had been, how the God of the Hebrews had put even him in his place, and how he'd been humbled by the experience. "But you, Belshazzar have not humbled yourself even you knew all this." And he proceeded to chastise Belshazzar publicly for his arrogance and pride. (**Daniel 5:22-24**)

Then he read the handwriting on the wall. Turns out it was written vertically, and the columns ran right to left. And as with all Aramiac, the vowels had to be assumed from the context. Without knowing the context it was next to impossible to insert the correct vowels, so between that and the vertical writing everyone was confused. Daniel understood because God gave him the insight.

The first two letters M and N were repeated and stood for mene, mene or in English "number, number." The next column to the left read TKL. Adding the vowels gave him the word Tekel or "weighed" in English. The final group of letters was PRS, and here Daniel inserted vowels and used the plural to make Parsin. Using the two available meanings of the word gave him "divided" and "Persians."

So these were the words. Mene, mene, tekel, parsin. Number, number, weighed, divided, Persians. With the wisdom of the Holy Spirit, Daniel translated it thus:

"God has numbered the days of your reign and brought it to an end (literally your number is up). You have been weighed on the scales and found wanting. Your kingdom is divided and given to the

Medes and Persians."

In spite of his earlier protestations, Daniel was immediately made the third ruler of Babylon. Later that night the Medes and Persians stormed through the gates and captured the city. Belshazzar was slain, but the city and its inhabitants were spared. The prophecy had been fulfilled.

Nearly 200 years earlier, before the city of Babylon was built or the king he named was born, Isaiah had prophesied that Cyrus the Persian would conquer this fortress city and told how it would be done. (**Isaiah 44:27-45:6**). The flow of the Euphrates would be temporarily diverted making the water level drop in Babylon and allowing a contingent of Persian soldiers to go under the bronze grates and open the city gates from the inside, thereby taking the city without a fight.

A few days after the Medo-Persian coalition captured Babylon, King Cyrus entered the city and was greeted by Daniel, now the ranking dignitary of the defeated Babylonians. Daniel showed him the portion of the scroll of Isaiah detailing his battle plan and written 200 years in advance. In the passage God called Cyrus "My Anointed" who would permit the rebuilding of Jerusalem and the release of the Jewish people from their captivity. This so impressed Cyrus that he made Daniel part of his senior governing staff. And true to the prophecy, Cyrus released the Jews, returned the stolen Temple implements, and gave them permission to go back to Jerusalem and begin rebuilding their Temple.

Several decades earlier, Jeremiah had prophesied

that the Babylonian captivity would last 70 years, at the end of which Babylon would be defeated and the Jewish people freed to return to Zion. (**Jere. 25:12 & 27:7**) Isaiah had told them who would do it and how, and Jeremiah had told them when it would happen. Both were right, for by the testimony of two witnesses a thing is established.

Now you know the adult version.

Daniel in the Lion's Den

Following about 70 years of absolute dominance over the known world, Babylon (Iraq) was conquered by a coalition of Persia (Iran) and Media (the Kurds) in about 538 BC. Thus began the rule of the Medo-Persian Empire, which lasted for 200 years or so until Alexander the Great conquered them.

The Beloved Prophet

Daniel had enjoyed God's favor all his life, and when Darius, the new King of Persia and son-in-law of Cyrus, appointed Daniel as one of 3 administrators to oversee the kingdom he so distinguished himself that Darius thought to give him sole administrative authority over all the kingdom. This of course made the others jealous and they sought to discredit him, but Daniel was trustworthy and neither corrupt nor negligent (**Dan 6:4**). Finally they devised a scheme to trap Daniel by making it illegal for him to worship God. They convinced Darius to make it mandatory for all his subjects to worship him for the next 30 days and anyone caught worshipping anyone else must be thrown into a den of hungry lions (**Dan 6:6-9**).

Daniel of course remained true to his God and since he made no attempt to hide this, he was caught praying to Him a few days later. When Darius was told, he was greatly distressed because he liked Daniel and made every effort to save him. But even he had to obey the law and so at sundown Darius was forced to give the order to have Daniel arrested. As he watched Daniel being lowered into the lions' den he said to him, "Your God whom you serve continually, He will deliver you." Then he sealed up the den, went home and, refusing to eat or be entertained, spent a sleepless night alone (**Dan 6:16-18**).

At dawn's first light, Darius hurried back to the lions' den and called out to Daniel "Has your God whom you serve continually been able to save you?" Daniel answered. "O King live forever. My God sent His angel, and he shut the lions' mouths. They have not hurt me because I was found innocent in His sight. Nor have I done anything wrong before you, O King"(**Dan 6:19-22**). Darius was overjoyed and gave the order to have Daniel lifted out of the lions' den. There was no wound or scratch on him because he had trusted God. Darius then had the men who had falsely accused Daniel rounded up and thrown into the lions' den along with their wives and children. Before they reached the floor of the den, the lions over powered them and crushed all their bones (**Dan 6:23-24**).

Testimony Time

Then Darius issued the following proclamation through out the land:

> May you prosper greatly. I issue a decree that in every part of my kingdom people must fear and reverence the God of Daniel.
>
> For He is the living God and He endures forever.
>
> His Kingdom will not be destroyed, His dominion will never end.
>
> He rescues and He saves, He performs signs and wonders in the heavens and on the earth.
>
> He has rescued Daniel from the power of the lions.

So Daniel prospered during the reign of Darius and the reign of Cyrus King of Persia.

What Do You Make Of That?

I think several important conclusions can de drawn:

1. From the original language of **Dan 6:16-20** it appears that Darius believed God was obligated to save Daniel because of the covenant that existed between them and was able to do so. He was anxious to see if God would be as faithful to the covenant as Daniel had been. I believe he had the lions' den sealed to keep the matter between Daniel and God; preventing Daniel's accusers from manipulating the outcome.

2. From his decree you could conclude that God's faithfulness to Daniel converted Darius, and prompted him to tell all his subjects about the power of the Living God to rescue those He loves and who have chosen Him (See **1 Thes. 1:9-10**). Knowing there's someone who's always faithful and true to His word is a powerful attraction to one who has been betrayed and abandoned, experiences I'm sure Darius suffered just as you and I have.

3. In **Dan 6:23** the word translated trusted means to trust continually. The fact that the lions immediately devoured Daniel's accusers in the morning proves they had been hungry all night long. The only time Daniel knew from experience that they wouldn't devour him was after he had been rescued. All through the dark night of captivity his had been a moment by moment series of contrary to feelings choices to believe God's promises in spite of his circumstances: to live by faith, not by sight (**2 Cor. 5:7**). This faith became one of the great examples in "The Hall of Faith" (**Hebrews 11:33**)

4. There's no indication that God had warned Daniel of these events in advance. But surely Daniel had read **2 Chron 16:9** "For the eyes of the Lord run to and fro through out the whole earth to show Himself strong in behalf of those whose heart is perfect toward Him." While we're cautioned not to put the Lord our God to the test (**Deut 6:16**), we also know that He who watches over Israel neither slumbers nor sleeps (**Ps 121:4**), and we can do all things

through Him who strengthens us (**Phil 4:13**). Our victories over the enemy become powerful tools for evangelism.

5. Daniel's night in the Lion's den portrays our life on earth. We're confined to this place and "our enemy the devil prowls around like a roaring lion looking for someone to devour" (**1 Ptr. 5:8**). But through faith we're shielded by God's power until the coming of (our) salvation that is ready to be revealed in the last time (**1 Ptr. 1:5**). Meanwhile our King Jesus knows that God is obligated to save us because of the covenant that exists between us and is able to do so (**Rom 8:38-39**). He will declare God's name to His brothers and in the congregation He will praise Him (**Ps 22:22**).

Now you know the adult version.

Jonah and the Whale

The Word of the Lord came to Jonah son of Amittai, "Go to the great city of Nineveh and preach against it because its wickedness has come up before me." (**Jonah 1:1-2**).

Jonah's name translates into English as dove and his father's name as truth, and Nineveh means progeny, so right away the story is intriguing to those of us who lean toward the mystical view. A dove showed Noah that God's judgment upon earth had truly ended and the flood waters were receding (**Gen.8:11**). Peace had been restored between the Creator and His creation. For the very poor, a dove was the prescribed offering for sin, restoring peace between the sinner and God (**Lev. 5:7**). The Spirit of the Lord descended upon Jesus "like a dove" in **Matt. 3:16** and we know that He came to restore peace between mankind and God (**Col. 1:19-20**). The story of Jonah involves restoring peace between the people of Nineveh and God and so it's fitting that He sent

Dove, the offspring of Truth to warn His progeny.

But Jonah ran away from the Lord and headed for Tarshish. (**Jonah 1:3**). Nineveh and Tarshish were at opposite ends of the known world. Nineveh was a great and wicked gentile city on the banks of the Tigris River in what's now Eastern Iraq, and Tarshish was either modern Spain or England depending on which commentator you read. I lean toward England since the Phoenicians traded extensively there and their name for the place roughly translates into Britannia. (This view also makes more sense to me in interpreting **Ezekiel 38:13**.)

But suffice it to say that God told Jonah to head east (Jonah came from the Galilee: **2 Kings 14:25**) and he booked passage on a boat heading west. By the way this little tidbit shows us how little the religious leaders of Jesus' day knew of the history of their prophets. In attempting to prove that Jesus couldn't be a prophet, they said, "A prophet does not come out of Galilee" (**John 7:25**) when in fact both Jonah and Nahum came from there. (The name of Peter's hometown Capernaum means village of Nahum.)

The Perfect Storm

On the voyage to Tarshish, they encountered a terrible storm, so bad it threatened to capsize the boat. Believing the storm to be sent from God, the sailors finally determined that Jonah was the reason for it, and so he asked them to throw him overboard. As soon as they did the storm subsided, and God sent a great fish that swallowed Jonah and kept him inside for 3 days and 3 nights (**Jonah 1:4-17**).

If you read chapter 2 literally and consult the original language you'll have to conclude that Jonah died and while his body remained inside the whale, his spirit went to Sheol, the abode of the dead. Sheol is a Hebrew word translated Hades in Greek, or Hell in English. It's located in the center of the Earth and before the cross, it's the place where every one went upon dying, because Jesus had not yet settled the sin problem once and for all.

Sheol was separated by a great chasm into two areas, a place of comfort for the faithful and a place of torment for those who had rejected God. The place of comfort was popularly called Paradise, or Abraham's bosom (**Luke 16:22-26**). When Jesus died, He went there and took the one crucified with Him who had asked Him to "Remember me when You come into Your Kingdom."(**Luke 23:42-43**)

When He rose from the grave He took the faithful dead with Him into Heaven (**Matt 27:53**) since His shed blood had finally erased the sins their sacrifices had only temporarily set aside. Since then all who die in faith go directly to be with the Lord (**Phil 1:22-23**).

Could I Try This Again?

While in Sheol Jonah asked for and received another chance to be faithful. The end of his prayer is remarkable in that it speaks of the Grace of God and declares the name of Jesus (Yeshua; translated Salvation comes from the Lord in **Jonah 2:8-9**.)

When the whale spit the resurrected Jonah onto dry ground, he went to Nineveh and began to preach, and was both astonished and angered when from the King on down those wicked gentiles immediately began to repent.

"I knew you would do this," he cried to God, "That's why I ran to Tarshish. I knew that You are a gracious and compassionate God, slow to anger and abounding in love" (**Jonah 4:1-2**). Then God caused a vine to grow and die as an object lesson to show Jonah that he was more concerned about the vine than about the people of Nineveh. After all, the vine brought him relief from the hot sun. What had the people of Nineveh done for him?

But remember, Nineveh means progeny. From God's point of view we are all His children, Jew and Gentile, saint and sinner, and deserving of a chance to repent and live. When we respond favorably, all is immediately forgiven and forgotten.

The Sign of The Prophet Jonah

When for the umpteenth time the Jews asked Jesus for a sign, He said no sign would be given except for the sign of the Prophet Jonah. "For as Jonah was 3 days and 3 nights in the belly of the huge fish, so the Son of Man will be 3 days and 3 nights in the belly of the Earth" (**Matt 12:40**). This reference validates Jonah's role as a prophet in Israel, verifies the accuracy of his story and points to the Lord's own resurrection. But what's the deeper meaning to all this?

First, Jonah is like all of us. Seeking God's grace for our own deliverance, we desire only justice for our enemies and are often angry when He shows them mercy. But the story of Jonah is also a parable of Israel and the Gentiles. Israel also failed in her first effort to fulfill her mission as God's witness (**Isa. 43:10-13**) and ceased to exist as a nation. And just as in Jonah's failure a boat load of sailors came to know the Lord and were saved (**Jonah 1:15-16**), so in Israel's failure a multitude of gentiles have come to know the Lord and be saved.

But Jonah returned from the dead and in his 2nd attempt the people of Nineveh repented and were spared from judgment to regain their lives. Israel has also returned from the dead. And in the remnant of Israel's faithfulness at the end of the age, more multitudes of God's progeny will repent and be spared from judgment to receive eternal life.

Now you know the adult version.

Coming Soon…

       Children's Stories of the Bible
            The Adult Version
                Vol. II
          The New Testament

Watch for it at…

               gracethrufaith.com

Breinigsville, PA USA
18 February 2010
232781BV00001B/3/A